THE

ESSENTIAL

CLASSICAL

RECORDINGS

— THE —
ESSENTIAL
CLASSICAL
RECORDINGS

101 CDs

RICK PHILLIPS

M&S

Library and Archives Canada Cataloguing in Publication

Phillips, Rick
The essential classical recordings : 101 CDs / Rick Phillips.

ISBN 0-7710-7001-2

1. Music–Discography. 2. Compact discs–Reviews. I. Title.

ML156.9.P562 2004   780.26'6   C2004-903239-9

We acknowledge the financial support of the Government of Canada
through the Book Publishing Industry Development Program and that
of the Government of Ontario through the Ontario Media Development
Corporation's Ontario Book Initiative. We further acknowledge the
support of the Canada Council for the Arts and the
Ontario Arts Council for our publishing program.

The lines on p. 230 are taken from the poem "Strange Meeting"
by Wilfred Owen, from *The Collected Poems of Wilfred Owen*,
copyright © 1963 by Chatto & Windus, Ltd.
Reprinted by permission of New Directions Publishing Corp.

Typeset in Janson by M&S, Toronto
Printed and bound in Canada

This book is printed on acid-free paper that is 100% recycled,
ancient-forest friendly (100% post-consumer recycled).

McClelland & Stewart Ltd.
The Canadian Publishers
481 University Avenue
Toronto, Ontario
M5G 2E9
www.mcclelland.com

1 2 3 4 5   08 07 06 05 04

To Hat who started it all,
and to Diane for love, support, and encouragement.

Handel

CONTENTS

THE
ESSENTIAL
CLASSICAL
RECORDINGS

INTRODUCTION

In the early seventeenth century, the English religious scholar Thomas Draxe said, "Music is the eye of the ear." The link to sight or the visual has been something music has wrestled with for generations. Today we tend to use our hearing as a way of confirming our sight, so Draxe's claim could easily be turned around to read, "Music is the ear of the eye." Manufactured images today are everywhere, in films, on television and computer screens, on billboards, and in the print media. We are now very visually oriented, relying on our sight to learn, experience, and entertain, and on our hearing to enhance what we see.

Since the development of radio and the gramophone in the twentieth century, music has lost ground to the visual in its power to arrest our attention. Music is in our homes and offices, and is as easily accessible as turning on the tap or the light switch. It's in elevators, dentist's offices, and shopping malls. Workers in factories often have music piped in to accompany their labours, but the music can't be too good, because then it can be distracting, and production targets fall. This ease of accessibility has caused us to take music for granted. We hear music constantly today, but we don't listen to it. It's used to fill a void, or a perceived void.

Yet music can still draw pictures and images for us. The great German Romantic writer Goethe is reported to have described architecture as frozen music. It's a powerful language that can communicate concepts and ideas non-visually and non-verbally, and it can also convey deep emotion and feeling.

This book is intended as a guide for both those who are just starting to explore the rich world of classical music and those who

already have a serious CD collection but want to explore other performances. It is, above all, for those who want to expand their aural
senses and awareness – who want to increase their understanding
and enjoyment of the highly useful and expressive language of
music. All forms of music are valid and worthy, from folk songs to
pop, jazz, rock, and hip hop. They can all express ideas and emotions. But this book deals with classical music – the age-old form
that has experienced many rises and falls over hundreds of years,
and still manages to survive. How we use music is up to each individual, but this book deals with music that was intended to be
listened to, not just heard – foreground listening, not background.

Today, we hear about the demise of the compact disc – the
format of recorded music that's been with us now for almost thirty
years. Downloads, MP3s, and soundfiles are the way of the future,
but, as always, the medium is not as important as the music.
Regardless of how we access it, it's the music itself that will
survive. Many of the classical music recordings recommended in
this book are "classic," and will always be available in one format
or another. Record companies are always reissuing recordings.
Every few years, they remaster the original tapes using the latest
technology, repackage them with new art, graphics, and jacket
notes, and re-release them. As a result, the serial numbers of the
recordings can change. But the music, artists, ensembles, and conductors remain the same, and usually the record label, so that's what
to look for. And remember that any list produced is obsolete the
minute it's printed. New recordings of classical music are always
coming out, but the recommendations in this book are recordings
that I think have a lasting shelf life.

Although there are 101 recommended recordings, you do not
have to acquire all of them to truly enjoy classical music. Used as
a guide, the book can steer you to furthering your own personal
musical tastes. I hope that it will also expose you to new insights
and ideas about music, encouraging you to listen to music that you
might not have thought you would ever enjoy. If you're like me,

you've sometimes been surprised at how your musical tastes have developed and changed over time, and how you're fond of music now that you would've never dreamed of liking a decade ago. I've attempted to supply an overview of classical music, ranging from the Middle Ages and before, to the present day. For the purposes of this book, the Middle Ages lead into the Renaissance, or the fifteenth and sixteenth centuries in music. The Baroque period is roughly 1600 to 1750. The Classical period of music runs from about 1750 to 1820 or so, overlapping with the nineteenth-century Romantic Age, and leading on into the modern age of the twentieth and twenty-first centuries.

I've avoided musical jargon and theoretical terms, and I don't think that it's necessary to be able to read music or understand musical theory or structure to enjoy classical music. They can enhance your appreciation, there's no question. But really, just an interest and an open mind are the first requirements to a life of musical enjoyment. Music is a non-verbal language. It shouldn't intimidate or scare anyone.

Many genres of music are here – from vocal and choral, to orchestral, chamber music, solo instrumental, and ballet. I've also tried to include a range of nationalities – not only of the composers, but also in the artists and ensembles selected. By no means is this a tally of the "best" 101 works or recordings. Any such list would be fruitless, given the subjectivity of art and music. It is simply an overview of classical music and recordings, and I don't make any claim that my selection is right or definitive, or even better than any other. But, over twenty-five years in the classical music business, as a writer, broadcaster, and teacher, I've been following what has been recorded and released, and its worth.

I've included just a few opera recordings. These recommendations are of composers whose operas affected the track of music, and therefore have a certain importance in the larger scheme of things. But when it comes to recordings, opera is an entire category of classical music unto itself, and couldn't be done true justice here.

Like any book of this type, there are bound to be omissions, some of which may jump out at you as you read. There's no music by Leoš Janáček, for example – the great Czech composer who straddled the nineteenth and twentieth centuries. But, given that I wanted to limit the book to 101 recommended recordings, I couldn't cover everything and everyone.

Throughout the planning and writing of the book, I kept price in mind. With the current flurry of reissues available today of good classical music recordings from the past, it is possible to acquire legendary recordings at great prices. But performers from the past are not necessarily the best. Living musicians like cellist Anner Bylsma or pianist Marc-André Hamelin are excellent by any standard. As it should be, price was only one factor, important as it may be. In the end, the recordings are recommended for a combination of worth and value.

Finally, to close, a quote by George Frideric Handel springs to mind, which is especially apt for a book on classical music and recordings. After the first performance of his oratorio *Messiah* in London, Handel is reported to have said, "I should be sorry if I have only succeeded in entertaining them. I wished to make them better."

GREGORIAN CHANT

In recent years, Gregorian chant has grown in popularity by leaps and bounds. Its simple, unadorned beauty has attracted many people looking for meaning and spirituality in today's hectic, materialistic world. Chant is a form of melodic prayer, and consequently it has a soothing, calming quality. Whether offering respite from a life of hard work, disease, and war a thousand years ago, or a moment of calm in today's stressful lives, Gregorian chant connects with people in a unique way. It creates an atmosphere of serenity and calm which only assists contemplation and relief.

Gregorian chant is the ancient collection of liturgical melodies of the Roman Catholic Church. Its name comes from Pope Gregory I, who reigned from 590 to 604, and was originally credited with developing it. Today, it's believed that Gregory's involvement (and that of his clergy) had more to do with collecting, cataloguing, and assigning the chant to specific liturgical occasions than it did with actually developing it. The problem with the designation "Gregorian," is that it ignores the existence of chant prior to the reign of Gregory I, as well as the changes, additions, and evolutions that took place later. For this reason, it's sometimes called Roman chant.

It probably originated in the Eastern Mediterranean, spreading westwards. There are elements of Jewish synagogue chant within it, as well as Greco-Roman and a host of other influences, which merged and evolved with Christian beliefs and philosophy. But most of the development then occurred in France, and was adopted in Rome by the thirteenth century.

Plainsong is another name sometimes used, but this now denotes a wider and more technical application today. Chant is a *Chant is* plain, un-harmonized melody with a rhythmic freedom that avoids a regular beat and metre. The rhythms stem from the natural accentuation and inflection of words and sentences. The tunes were indicated by neumes, or small signs and instructions to the singers, notated above the words. It could be sung solo by the cantor, or chorally, but in both cases it was monophonic, or having a single line of music. As time went on, polyphonic music developed, or music with two or more individual lines. Chant then seemed crude and primitive, and it was often harmonized with the addition of instrumental accompaniments. This was believed to have improved it. Thankfully, today the ancient tradition has been restored and this music has a new life, after centuries of neglect and harmful treatments.

The recommended recording features Gregorian chant for the various festivals of the church year. The monks of the Benedictine abbey of Münsterschwarzach create a balanced and blended sound, with phrases that rise and fall without hard attacks or peaks, and where the last syllable is always softened. Their diction is clear, enhancing the free, naturally inflected rhythms of speech. But it's not all dreamy and atmospheric. This is singing with a youthful freshness that provides contemplation and spirituality within a robust approach to everyday life. The spacious but clean recorded sound only adds to the experience.

■

GREGORIAN CHANT: *Great Festivals of the Church Year*
Münsterschwarzach Benedictine Abbey Choir/
    Father Godehard Joppich
DGG Eloquence   469 655-2

JOSQUIN DESPREZ (c.1440–1521): *"L'homme armé" Masses*

One of the greatest composers of the Renaissance was Josquin Desprez, but very little is known about his life. He's believed to have been born in the region of Picardy in France sometime around 1440, and it's possible that he studied with the great Flemish master, Joannes Ockeghem. The name Josquin appears as a singer in the Cathedral in Milan in 1459. He probably spent some time in Milan, then Florence, before arriving in Rome in the mid-1480s as a member of the papal choir. By 1501, he had left Italy and returned to France, where he likely worked for the court of King Louis XII. At one point, it seems he was employed at the court of the Duke of Ferrara, but fled at the outbreak of the plague in 1503. Josquin's position was taken by Flemish composer Jacob Obrecht, who succumbed to the plague in 1505. For the rest of his life, Josquin worked in the north at a church in Condé-sur-l'Escaut, where he died in 1521. Several portraits of him have survived the centuries, one of them attributed to Leonardo da Vinci.

After his death, Josquin's fame rose as his music became better known throughout Europe, through printing and reprintings. Many younger musicians claimed to have studied with him. He left a large body of work – probably more than any major composer before him, and in many forms and genres. Josquin took the art of polyphony, or multiple independent parts, to a new level, adding a lyrical beauty to it that it had never known, within an economy of means. His music is a synthesis of the counterpoint of the Flemish style of the north, and the more harmonically oriented music of Italy. Josquin was the favourite composer of Martin Luther, who called him "the supreme master of the notes." Luther went on in his praise, saying, "the notes must express whatever Josquin wants them to, whereas other composers can only do what the notes demand."

"L'homme armé" was a popular song that may have originated with the Crusades. A translation of the words to the song are:

> Beware the armed man. Word has gone out that everyone should arm himself with a haubregon of iron [a coat of mail]. Beware the armed man.

Composers of the period usually based their polyphonic mass settings on ancient plainchant tunes. But the song "L'homme armé" was also used as the basic musical material for masses for about two centuries, by just about every composer you can name. In the Renaissance alone, over thirty mass settings used the song, among them the two by Josquin that are included on the recommended recording. The tradition of using "L'homme armé" as the building block for a mass ended in the seventeenth century with Carissimi.

The Tallis Scholars under their founding director, Peter Phillips, are one of the finest choirs working. They specialize in a cappella Renaissance polyphonic music, and their many recordings have increased the interest, and love, for this great genre of choral music. The group produces a wonderful sound – blended, balanced, and proportioned but with each line clearly defined and with pure intonation. Female sopranos are used instead of boys, but with a sound like this, only those craving the most authentic performances will be bothered by the substitution. There's a love, enthusiasm, and ease in recordings by the Tallis Scholars that comes across in their consistently strong recordings, many of them award-winners.

JOSQUIN DESPREZ: *L'homme armé Masses*
The Tallis Scholars/Peter Phillips
Gimell Records   CDGIM 019

GIOVANNI DA PALESTRINA (c.1525–1594):
Pope Marcellus Mass

The sixteenth-century Italian composer Giovanni Pierluigi da Palestrina is known today simply as Palestrina after the small town of his birth, about thirty kilometres from Rome. He was born there in 1525, the son of a landowner, and grew up comfortably. As a boy, Palestrina sang in the local church choir. When the Bishop of Palestrina was summoned to Rome to become an archbishop around 1534, he took the boy with him. There, Palestrina received musical training and continued to be a chorister. Then he returned to his hometown to take on a job as organist for a few years, and married. When, around 1550, the Bishop of Palestrina was elected Pope Julius III, Palestrina returned to Rome, this time to direct the Julian Choir at St. Peter's. Shortly afterward, Palestrina was appointed by the pope to the choir of the Sistine Chapel, which created considerable ire among the other singers. Palestrina did not possess a very pleasing singing voice, he was married, and he got the position without having to take the prerequisite examinations or undergo the scrutiny of his peers. There hadn't even been a vacancy in the choir! It's not surprising that after Pope Julius III died in 1555, a successor, Paul IV, had Palestrina removed from the choir.

By 1570, Palestrina had become one of the most famous composers in Europe. His music was widely distributed, and he was frequently offered jobs. After the death of his first wife, he married the wealthy heiress of a furrier. For the rest of his life, Palestrina combined his musical activities with running the fur shop. He died in Rome in 1594.

Palestrina probably composed his *Missa Papae Marcelli* in 1556. The work is named after Pope Marcellus II, who reigned for only three weeks during 1555. At this time the Roman Catholic Church was still reeling from the blows of the Reformation. The church wanted to reform itself to prevent further heresy, and the Council of Trent was set up to look into the matter. One of the things to be considered was the music of the church, as Pope Marcellus believed that church music had become unintelligible and too secular. Polyphonic music didn't allow for the text to be understood, and the use of secular tunes (like "L'homme armé" – see the entry on Josquin) as the basis of the material was too profane. The story goes that the church fathers were considering banning all polyphonic music and returning to plainchant, or monophonic music, when Palestrina composed his Pope Marcellus Mass and convinced them that music of dignity and nobility could still be written in the polyphonic style, and that the words could be clearly understood. Thus, Palestrina "saved" music from returning to its roots. Today, much of this story is considered apocryphal, but it was used as the basis for a 1917 opera called *Palestrina* by the German composer Hans Pfitzner (1869–1949). In it, Pfitzner contrasts the trials of mundane, everyday life with artistic genius. Regardless of the reasons for its existence, the Pope Marcellus Mass has survived because of its high quality, exhibiting Palestrina's skill in combining technical craft and devotion into music of great beauty.

The members of the sixteenth-century Council of Trent would have enjoyed the recording of the Pope Marcellus Mass by the Tallis Scholars under Peter Phillips. The purity of tone and the clarity of the individual lines are exemplary, and the words can be clearly understood. But there's also a wonderful momentum, that always pushes forward, well-paced and never rushed. The recording contains a full acoustic, without muddying the textures or texts.

GIOVANNI DA PALESTRINA: *Pope Marcellus Mass*
The Tallis Scholars/Peter Phillips
Gimell   CDGIM 339

CLAUDIO MONTEVERDI (1567–1643):
Vespro della Beata Vergine (1610 Vespers)

The life of Claudio Monteverdi bridged the sixteenth and seventeenth centuries, and his music, too, linked the huge stylistic differences in music between the two eras. He was born in 1567 in the Italian town of Cremona, sometimes known as the "City of Violins" because of the great violin-makers – Amati, Guarneri, and Stradivari – who practised their craft there. Monteverdi's career can be divided into three periods. He spent his first twenty years in Cremona, where he studied and published his first music. Early influences were the Franco-Flemish composers, men such as Dufay, Ockeghem, and Josquin. At the age of twenty, Monteverdi was clearly a talented composer with great potential, who seemed eager to spread his wings and try new musical ideas.

Monteverdi's second period begins around 1590, when he was hired by the Gonzaga Court in Mantua. Vincenzo Gonzaga, Duke of Mantua, was rich, snobbish, hedonistic, arrogant, ostentatious, and extremely powerful and influential. Over two hundred and fifty years later, the character of the Duke shows up in the opera *Rigoletto* by Giuseppe Verdi, based on a play by Victor Hugo. But despite his character flaws, the Duke of Mantua loved art and music, and used them as symbols of his wealth and status. At his court, he had his own chapel and theatre, with a full complement of actors, designers, painters, directors, musicians, and composers. The great Flemish painter Peter Paul Rubens was on staff at one point. Monteverdi became the *maestro di cappella*, or music director of the court in 1601, but the job was far from ideal. He complained of overwork, poor pay, and being taken for granted. "I know one can compose fast, but fast and good do not go well together," he once wrote. Monteverdi became so frustrated that at one point, he submitted a letter of resignation and returned to Cremona. The Duke ordered him to return to Mantua, and Monteverdi obliged, but in a roundabout way looking for a new job.

Then in 1612, the Duke died, and his successor was not as interested in art and music. Monteverdi either resigned or was let go. His third and final period begins the following year, in 1613, when he was offered the dream job of *maestro di cappella* at St. Mark's Basilica in Venice. At the time, Venice was one of the most cosmopolitan cities in Europe – liberal, democratic, wealthy, and prominent. It was very advanced musically, and Monteverdi's job was well-paid and gave him prestige and freedom – and an apartment. Much of the music he composed for St. Mark's was sacred, but Monteverdi always was fascinated by secular music, like madrigals and opera. With a new opera house in Venice, he was encouraged to compose one dramatic work after another, many of them lost today. He died in Venice in 1643, a respected and admired musician.

Monteverdi published the *Vespro della Beata Vergine*, or "Vespers of the Blessed Virgin" in 1610. Today, they are often simply called the "1610 Vespers." At the time, he was unhappily employed at the Gonzaga Court in Mantua. By 1610, things had become almost intolerable, and it's believed Monteverdi composed the vespers as a potential ticket out of Mantua. The work is flatteringly dedicated to Pope Paul v. Monteverdi exhibited his skill in both the old and new styles of music in the 1610 Vespers. He was completely comfortable going from the *stile antico* of modes, polyphony, and chant of the sixteenth century and earlier, to the major/minor tonalities, homophony, and dance-like instrumental music of the seventeenth century. If his intent was to demonstrate his versatility in a wide range of musical styles, he was very successful. It's believed that Monteverdi's appointment at

St. Mark's in Venice in 1613, was due, at least in part, to the 1610 Vespers. And it's likely that Monteverdi never actually intended the vespers to be performed as a whole. Given their grand scale and the huge performing forces required, it's quite probable that he meant the work as a presentation volume and not for ordinary use at the time.

William Christie and his group, Les Arts Florissants, have been presenting strong performances and recordings of early music for over twenty-five years. This 1997 recording of Monteverdi's 1610 Vespers is rich, glorious, and warm. Christie brings out the variety of texture and sonorities in the work, clearly showing Monteverdi's genius in combining the old style with the new. Soloists, choir, and orchestra perform superbly, with a good sense of drama and vitality, making this one of the great recordings of this landmark piece of music.

■────────────────────────────────────

CLAUDIO MONTEVERDI: *Vespro della Beata Vergine (1610)*
Les Arts Florissants/William Christie
Erato   3984-23139-2

ARCANGELO CORELLI (1653–1713):
Violin Sonatas, Op. 5

Like too many composers throughout music history, Arcangelo Corelli was much more famous in his day than he is now. Today, he is known for one or two works – the Concerto Grosso, Op. 6, No. 8, known as his "Christmas Concerto," intended to honour the night of Christ's nativity, and the Violin Sonata Op. 5, No. 12, known as "La Folia" because of the ancient stately dance on which the sonata is based. But, at the turn into the eighteenth century, there were few composers as celebrated in Europe as Corelli, and his stature lasted well into the nineteenth century, often eclipsing both Bach and Handel. The sheer volume of the printing and reprinting of his music attests to his fame. His set of twelve Violin Sonatas, Op. 5, was first published in 1700. By 1800, at least forty-two editions of the set had appeared, and that doesn't include the countless arrangements and borrowings by other composers. The Op. 5 Violin Sonatas are some of the finest in the repertoire, and they influenced many composers who followed. If imitation is the greatest form of flattery, this is especially true of Corelli, although his imitators rarely acknowledged their debt to him.

What was so groundbreaking about the Op. 5 Violin Sonatas is their idiomatic treatment. Prior to this, composers tended to write parts that could feasibly be played on a variety of instruments. Composing the music with the idiosyncrasies of particular instruments in mind was new. Corelli wrote music to which only the instruments for which he composed could adequately give the proper effect. As you can imagine, this was a huge step forward in the development of instrumental music.

From all reports, Corelli was a simple, modest man who lived frugally, despite his considerable wealth. His dress and behaviour were conservative, bordering on shabby. Other than music, his passion was art and sculpture, and at his death, he left a large collection, mostly by Romans, but including one Breughel. Yet he never permitted himself the luxury of attending an art gallery on days when admission was charged. His conservative, modest deportment was in variance with his performing style. According to one eyewitness, when performing, Corelli was quite expressive. "His eyes will sometimes turn as red as fire, his countenance will be distorted, and his eyeballs roll as in an agony!"

As well as being a gifted violinist and composer, Corelli was also an exceptional and very influential teacher. His students came from far and wide – from Italy, Germany, France, Spain, and England. One of the most famous was the violinist and composer Francesco Geminiani (1687–1762), who nicely summed up his teacher this way: "Corelli's merit was not depth of learning, nor great fancy or rich invention in melody or harmony, but a nice ear and most delicate taste which led him to select the most pleasing harmonies and melodies and to construct the parts so as to produce the most delightful effect upon the ear."

Violinist Andrew Manze and harpsichordist Richard Egarr are two of today's finest Baroque musicians, with a proven track record. They are able to transform the notes on the page into wonderful musical experiences, combining elegance and detail with spontaneity and improvisation. Texture, clarity, and variety are always front and centre, and as a result, this recording presents the Op. 5 Violin Sonatas by Corelli as the true masterpieces they are.

■───

ARCANGELO CORELLI: *Violin Sonatas, Op. 5*
Andrew Manze, Richard Egarr
Harmonia Mundi   HMU 907298/9

HENRY PURCELL (1659–1695):
Ode for St. Cecilia's Day

Between the time of the Elizabethan lute songs composed by John Dowland and the works of the early twentieth-century composer Sir Edward Elgar, there weren't many native-born English composers. Sir Arthur Sullivan, Sir Charles Hubert Parry, and Sir Charles Villiers Stanford are worthy exceptions, but music in England was often spearheaded by continental European composers. Handel was a German-born, Italian-trained musician who made his name in England in the eighteenth century. Felix Mendelssohn, another German, had a long and close association with England in the first part of the nineteenth century, becoming a favourite of both Queen Victoria and her husband, Prince Albert.

Henry Purcell stands out from this pattern. He was an English-born composer whose genius stemmed from his ability to absorb what was going on musically around him, and assimilate it into his own music. In his theatre music, Purcell blended French and Italian influences; his church music bears the stamp of the great English choral tradition that preceded him; his sonatas illustrate his knowledge of the Italian instrumental masters; and his chamber music often harks back to earlier English consort music.

Purcell came to his craft honourably. His father had been a distinguished musician and a Gentleman of the Chapel Royal to King Charles II. Henry likely received his early music training from his father, and followed in his footsteps. At about age ten, he became a chorister at the Chapel Royal, but left when his voice broke in 1673. Purcell was then appointed "keeper, maker, mender, repairer, and tuner of the King's Instruments," a job that paid thirty pounds a year, with an allowance for wardrobe. He tuned the organ at Westminster Abbey, and made some money as a copyist. In 1679, he was appointed Organist at Westminster Abbey, in addition to the position of composer to the King's Violins. Then, beginning about 1680, Purcell became more and more interested in the theatre. He wrote quite a bit of incidental music to plays, as well as numerous other stage works, the culmination being his opera *Dido and Aeneas.*

One of Purcell's gifts was his facility in setting the English language to music. English is often a difficult language to sing, but Purcell successfully adapted the natural inflections of speech into his music. "The melodies seem to float on the words," was how one English scholar explained it.

Purcell worked hard all his life, and his death in 1695 in his mid-thirties was probably due to a combination of tuberculosis and exhaustion. He is buried in Westminster Abbey, and on a tablet near the grave is the following inscription: "Here lyes Henry Purcell, Esq., who left this life and is gone to that Blessed Place where only his harmony can be exceeded."

His friend and collaborator, the poet and dramatist John Dryden wrote an ode in memory to Purcell that includes the lines,

Sometimes a hero in an age appears,
But scarce a Purcell in a thousand years.

Purcell composed several pieces of music for performance on November 22 – St. Cecilia's Day, the patron saint of music. (He died on the eve of St. Cecilia's Day.) The ode "Hail Bright Cecilia" was written for the 1692 celebrations, and is his longest non-theatrical work. This recording of it, which also includes the verse anthems "My Beloved Spake" and "O Sing Unto the Lord," was released for the tercentenary of Purcell's death in 1995. Paul McCreesh and the Gabrieli Consort & Players present a brilliant account with some excellent solo singing. Grandeur and pomp are

beautifully matched with intimacy and insight. At times, it's difficult to realize that the choir here numbers under twenty members.
The richness of Purcell's range of colours and textures, and his
imagination in melody, harmony, and rhythm have rarely been
better achieved.

HENRY PURCELL: *Ode for St. Cecilia's Day*
The Gabrieli Consort & Players/Paul McCreesh
Archiv Blue   471 728-2

ANTONIO VIVALDI (1678–1741):
The Four Seasons

The four violin concertos by Antonio Vivaldi known as "The Four Seasons" are some of the most popular pieces in classical music. And to many music lovers, Vivaldi is known mainly as a composer of concertos. It's sometimes said that Vivaldi wrote one concerto five hundred times. But this is unfair, and any lover of Vivaldi can appreciate that every concerto by him is unique. No less a musician than the great Johann Sebastian Bach held Vivaldi in very high regard and even transcribed several of his works. In recent years, Vivaldi's magnificent operas have begun to be performed and recorded more often, and the view of him strictly as an instrumental composer has started to change.

Vivaldi's Op. 8, consisting of twelve concertos, was published in 1725 under the title *Il cimento dell'armonia e dell'inventione*, or *The Contest Between Harmony and Invention*. By this title, it's believed that Vivaldi meant to show the conflict that exists in the mind of a composer when he tries to balance the form and structure of music with the imagination; its science and logic with fantasy. The first four concertos of Op. 8 are the ones known as "The Four Seasons," and depict the different seasons of the year, beginning with spring and ending with winter. At the top of each of the concertos, Vivaldi included a short sonnet with descriptive features of each of the seasons, probably written by him. He was clearly a much better composer than a poet, but nevertheless, the sonnets do provide a hint to the conflict in music between the rational and the imaginative or programmatic. The question has always lingered, though, whether Vivaldi composed the sonnets first, and then the music to match, or the music first, followed by the accompanying sonnet. Regardless of which came first, we can clearly hear in the music the singing of birds in spring, the goatherd's barking dog, thunder and lightning, and a frigid, shivering winter landscape.

Despite these programmatic links and devices, Vivaldi composed in the strict forms of the solo Baroque concerto. The layout of the movements is the standard fast-slow-fast, with the outer movements flashy and virtuosic, while the middle movement is more lyrical and abstract. The musical material is usually presented by the orchestra, followed by the solo violin.

Vivaldi's "The Four Seasons" is one of the most often-recorded works of all time, and the possibilities of style and approach are almost limitless, from full-blown symphony orchestras to small period instrument ensembles. The 1984 BIS recording with violinist Nils-Erik Sparf and the Drottningholm Baroque Ensemble from Sweden is one of the most imaginative in bringing across the descriptions supplied by Vivaldi without ever overdoing it. The musicians always seem to keep in mind Vivaldi's idea of the contest between harmony and invention, and the necessary balance that's required. There's also a youthful freshness and energy to the playing, as if this were the very first time any of them had played, or heard this music.

■

ANTONIO VIVALDI: *The Four Seasons*
Nils-Erik Sparf, Drottningholm Baroque Orchestra
BIS CD-275

JEAN-PHILIPPE RAMEAU (1683–1764):
Overtures & Suites

Until the last few decades, the name Jean-Philippe Rameau was little known – he was yet another obscure composer in the annals of music history. But today, largely through the championing of members of the Early Music movement, Rameau has emerged as one of the most important figures in Baroque music. He was really the French counterpart of his German contemporary, Johann Sebastian Bach. And like Bach, Rameau took the musical traits and styles of the Baroque period to their apex.

Rameau came from Dijon, the son of a church organist who followed in his father's footsteps. He spent a year studying in Italy as a teenager, and when he returned to France in 1702, he concentrated on composing music for the church, the organ, and the harpsichord. The short pieces in Rameau's books of harpsichord pieces are often dances like gavottes, minuets, and gigues, with witty, descriptive titles like "La Poule," "La Chasse," or "Les Triolets."

Rameau moved to Paris in the early 1720s, where he remained for the rest of his life. He was interested in all aspects of music and in 1722 he published a theoretical treatise that, even today, remains an important document. In it, Rameau laid out the concepts of harmony and their applications, strongly influencing generations of musicians that followed. Rameau is just as important a musical theorist as he is a composer.

But for a long time his dream was to compose for the stage. Finally at the age of fifty, Rameau presented his opera *Hippolyte et Aricie*. It created quite a commotion, drawing screams of rage from the disciples of Jean-Baptiste Lully, the earlier Italian-born French composer, who is often credited with founding French opera. To the Lullists, Rameau's music was too complex and cerebral and placed too much emphasis on drama and orchestration, and not enough on lyricism. A popular verse at the time took Rameau to task:

If the difficulty is pretty,
What a great man Rameau is!
But if, by chance, what e'er is witty
must be simple, then I know
He is but a little man.

These musical factions continued to bicker, and the squabble came to a head in 1752 in "la guerre des bouffons" or the "War of the Buffoons," initiated by a performance of an opera by Pergolesi, put on in Paris by a touring Italian company. Rameau found himself on the conservative side. But he emerged victorious from "la guerre," and his principles of French opera were finally accepted, and enjoyed, by French opera lovers.

As well as sets, costumes, and singers, eighteenth-century French opera also included instrumental dances. Rameau brought a new, wider range of feelings and moods to his dances, employing a constantly changing variety of orchestral textures and sonorities.

The recommended recording features instrumental overtures and suites from several of Rameau's stage works, including *Castor et Pollux*, *Les Indes galantes*, and one of his last operas, *Les Paladins*. The conductors Raymond Leppard, Gustav Leonhardt, and Frans Brüggen are all somewhat responsible for the current popularity of music from the French Baroque. They lead performances that are spirited and lively, and the orchestras delight in the colours and rhythms of these innovative and imaginative scores.

■

JEAN-PHILIPPE RAMEAU: *Overtures & Suites*
Orchestra of the 18th Century, Orchestra of the Age of
Enlightenment, New Philharmonia Orchestra/Frans Brüggen,
Gustav Leonhardt, Raymond Leppard
Philips Eloquence 468 169-2

JOHANN SEBASTIAN BACH (1685–1750):
The Brandenburg Concertos

In 1717, Johann Sebastian Bach was appointed *Kapellmeister* (music director) at the small court of Prince Leopold of Cöthen. The prince was a keen amateur musician himself, played several instruments quite well, and had a good orchestra on-site. The court of Cöthen was Calvinist, not Lutheran – a sect that frowned upon the use of music in church – so most of the music that Bach was required to compose in his years in Cöthen was instrumental and orchestral.

In 1719, Bach travelled to Berlin, the Prussian capital, to purchase a new harpsichord and while there, he performed for Christian Ludwig, the Margrave of Brandenburg, another avid music lover. On his leave, the Margrave informally asked Bach to send him some of his music. The request was pretty loose, and Bach took a couple of years to fulfill it. He reworked and modified six concertos that he had probably written for use in Cöthen, and sent them to the Margrave in Berlin in 1721. On the title page, in the dedication to the Margrave, Bach wrote the following, providing a good sense of the status of the composer in the early eighteenth century:

> I have taken the liberty of rendering my most humble duty to Your Royal Highness with the present concertos . . . begging Your Highness most humbly not to judge their imperfections with the rigour of the fine and delicate taste which the whole world knows Your Highness has for musical pieces; but rather to infer from them in benign consideration the profound respect and the most humble obedience which I try to show Your Highness herewith.

The six Brandenburg Concertos by Bach are textbook examples of the Baroque form of the *concerto grosso*. In it, the composer pitted two contrasting groups of instruments against each other. A small group of solo instruments was called the *concertino*, while the larger group was known as the *ripieno*. For example, in the Brandenburg Concerto No. 2, the concertino is made up of trumpet, recorder, oboe, and violin, while the ripieno is the orchestra of strings and *continuo* (usually harpsichord and cello). The variety of permutations and combinations that could be created with the different instruments and groups fascinated both the Baroque composer and music lover. The musicians involved could be assigned solo and supporting roles, and a variety of sonorities, textures, methods, and styles could be achieved. But Bach, who was very aware of the musical goings-on across Europe at the time, also combined the Italian form with French grace and elegance and the craft of German polyphonic writing. No two of the six Brandenburg Concertos are alike, and as a set, they are the culmination of the Baroque concerto grosso.

A recording of the Brandenburg Concertos, played on period instruments by The English Concert under the direction of Trevor Pinnock, has been highly recommended since its original release over twenty years ago. Rhythms are crisp and dance-like, energy and spirits are high, while the slow movements have a depth of emotion and expression. The clear recording and excellent performance standards easily show Bach's mastery of the concerto grosso form, as well as his creativity and musical imagination.

J.S. BACH: *The Brandenburg Concertos*
The English Concert/Trevor Pinnock
Archiv Blue 471 720-2

JOHANN SEBASTIAN BACH (1685–1750):
The Six Suites for Solo Cello

Much of the chamber music by J.S. Bach comes from his time at the court at Cöthen, between 1717 and 1723. Prince Leopold of Cöthen was a keen music lover and a good amateur musician on several instruments. Although Bach composed his six suites for solo cello in Cöthen, they probably were not intended for the prince to play. If he did have a performer in mind, he remains unknown. With no known precedents for this music, the question arises, why did Bach compose them?

The six solo cello suites are further examples of Bach's astonishing skills as a composer. It's likely that he simply enjoyed the challenge of writing music for a single instrument without any accompaniment. Where other composers ponder how many instruments to use, Bach here seems to be asking, "How many instruments can I take away, and still make music work?" The essential musical elements of melody, harmony, and rhythm have never been combined as simply, or as well.

A suite is a selection of dance movements. By the early eighteenth century, it had become standard to include an *allemande*, a *courante*, a slow *sarabande*, and a fast *gigue*, or jig. For his solo cello suites, Bach opened each one with an introductory prelude before the allemande. Then between the sarabande and the gigue, he inserted a pair of additional dances, either minuets, bourrées or gavottes. The toe-tapping gigues then closed each suite.

As the suites progress, they become more difficult for the cellist. For Suite No. 5, the cellist is instructed to tune the instrument's high A string down a tone to G, changing the tone quality and making it darker. The Suite No. 6 is the most difficult as it has a lot of high passage work, suggesting that it was written for a cello with an additional string. These differences have led scholars to speculate that the Suites Nos. 5 and 6 may have been composed at another time.

Although the cello is able to play more than one note at a time (through double-stopping), it is essentially a single line instrument. At first hearing, this music, as it is without any accompaniment, can sound exposed and stark. Our ears are just not used to the open and austere sound of a single cello. The genius is how Bach gets around this limitation by suggesting or implying harmonies and textures. A good example is the Prelude to the Suite No. 1. This is simply a series of chords, but instead of being played together, the notes making up the chords are played separately. The result is a soothing forward drive supplied by the separated notes, but with the harmony implied. In listening to the suites, we shouldn't be as concerned with what's not there, as we should with what *is* there.

The Dutch cellist Anner Bylsma is the dean of Baroque period instrument cellists. His light, lean sound gives the suites great delicacy and enhances many of the dance characteristics of the movements. With none of the hearty *woofs* that the cello can produce when the player digs into it with the bow, Bylsma plays gently, offering fresh insights into this ageless music.

■ ⎯⎯⎯⎯⎯⎯⎯⎯⎯⎯⎯⎯⎯⎯⎯⎯⎯⎯⎯⎯⎯⎯

J.S. BACH: *The Six Suites for Solo Cello*
Anner Bylsma
Sony Classical   S2K 48047

JOHANN SEBASTIAN BACH (1685–1750):
The Goldberg Variations

The Goldberg Variations by Bach is one of the keyboard pinnacles of the variation technique of composition. The story goes that Bach composed the work on commission from Count Keyserlingk, the Russian ambassador to the Court of Saxony in Dresden. The count was a chronic insomniac and asked Bach for some keyboard pieces that would soothe him and help him drop off to sleep. Johann Gottlieb Goldberg was one of Bach's students, and the count's keyboard player. It was likely Goldberg who played the variations for the count. Hence the title.

The Goldberg Variations begins with the statement of a simple but ornamented song-like theme. Bach then subjects that theme to a total of thirty variations, organized into ten groups of three variations each. The range and approach of each variation conjured up by Bach is another example of his strong interest in pedagogy. The Goldbergs is a syllabus or specimen book by Bach on how to compose in the variation technique. But the work is also a wonderful example of the scope and variety of Baroque keyboard technique, with no two variations even similar. After the thirty variations, Bach repeats the original theme. The effect is calming, making listeners feel as if they have returned home after a long journey. But heard after all the variations, this time the theme sounds quite different. We've come to know it better through the variations, and it can never again sound quite like the original.

Canadian pianist Glenn Gould began and finished his career with the Goldberg Variations. For his 1955 recording debut with CBS he played the Goldbergs. Record company executives frowned at the suggestion of a young pianist in his twenties making his debut with what seemed like a stodgy, pedagogical work. Chopin or Rachmaninoff was more to their thinking. But Gould insisted, and the result was a stunning recording that caught the record-buying public by storm. Gould and the Goldberg Variations were rocketed to stardom. He later retired from public performance to devote his time to recording, writing, radio documentaries, and other interests. But then in 1981, Gould returned to the Goldberg Variations for another crack at it. Both he and recording technology had changed in the intervening twenty-five years, and he felt that he had something new to say. It too was a top-seller, but it was one of the last recordings Gould made. He died in 1982 at the age of fifty.

The Sony Classical set titled *Glenn Gould – A State of Wonder* was released in 2002, the seventieth anniversary of Gould's birth, and the twentieth anniversary of his death. For the first time, both the 1955 and the 1981 Gould recordings of the Goldberg Variations were available together on CD. The contrast in Gould's approach is clear. The 1955 recording is youthful and fresh, even brash, the 1981 recording is slower and more searching, with deeper humanity and emotion. Both interpretations are valid, both show a pianist of rare skill and insight. Also included is a radio interview with Gould by music critic Tim Page, where the two versions are compared. And there are a number of outtakes from the 1955 studio session that offer further insight into the Goldberg Variations, as well as Glenn Gould the pianist and the man.

J.S. BACH: *The Goldberg Variations – A State of Wonder (1955, 1981)*
Glenn Gould
Sony Classical S3K 87703

JOHANN SEBASTIAN BACH (1685–1750): *The St. Matthew Passion*

J.S. Bach spent the last twenty-seven years of his life as Cantor in Leipzig. He was responsible for much of the town's musical business, composing the music for the churches and other outlets, as well as teaching. It had been the tradition in Leipzig to perform a Passion every year on Good Friday, and Bach was expected to continue the tradition. He probably composed five Passions in Leipzig, but only two have survived intact: The *St. John Passion* and the *St. Matthew Passion.*

A Passion is a work performed during Holy Week for vocal soloists, choir, and orchestra that deals with the story of the crucifixion of Christ, according to one of the gospels in the Bible: Matthew, Mark, Luke, or John. It contains recitatives, arias, duets, and choruses. The Lutheran Passions also included chorales, or hymns, used as punctuation points throughout, that reflect on what was happening in the story.

The *St. Matthew Passion* by Bach came after the *St. John*, and is believed to have been first performed at the Church of St. Thomas in Leipzig on Good Friday, 1727, with Bach directing. The text was taken from chapters 26 and 27 of the gospel according to St. Matthew, with additional words supplied by Picander, the pen name of Christian Friedrich Henrici. Picander was a good poet whose day job was with the postal service in Leipzig, and Bach turned quite often to him for Passion and cantata texts. The *St. Matthew Passion* by Bach was probably performed two or three times again in Leipzig, during the composer's lifetime. Then, as musical tastes changed and the Rococo and Classical periods got underway, the work fell into obscurity. Bach's music was considered old-fashioned and the work was probably not heard again publicly for a century, until Felix Mendelssohn put on a performance of it in Berlin in 1829. The *St. Matthew Passion*, and the music of Bach, were rediscovered and have continued to grow in popularity ever since.

The *St. Matthew Passion* is huge in conception, requiring double choir, double orchestra, a boys' choir, and several soloists. A tenor sings the part of the Evangelist – in this case St. Matthew, telling the story. A bass takes the role of Jesus, who, for most of the work, is accompanied by soft, chordal strings – a "halo" of strings that makes him stand out from the other characters. The Passion story is told through the recitatives, with help from the chorus, which sometimes plays the role of biblical crowds. The emotion of the story comes across in the arias and duets, where feelings and meditations on Jesus' death are reflected by vocal soloists. The chorales are used to pause and reflect on the action. In Bach's time, the chorales, and their meaning, would have been immediately recognized by the congregation. It's possible that the congregation joined in.

Typical of Bach, the text is magnificently set, with much use of symbolism and numerology. For example, in the scene of the Last Supper, Christ warns that he will be betrayed by one of the disciples. Bach has the chorus sing the question, "Lord, is it I?" eleven times – once for each of the disciples except Judas.

The *St. Matthew Passion* by Bach is one of the great works of art, not just musical art. It's a brilliantly conceived example of the capabilities of the human mind when inspired – a work of incredible richness and complexity that continues to reveal its mysteries in repeated hearings.

The Harmonia Mundi recording directed by Philippe Herreweghe stands out for several reasons. First of all, Howard Crook as the Evangelist is brilliant in his telling of the Passion story. He's dramatic, expressing warmth, solace, passion, and sympathy in a highly musical style. The soloists, choirs, and orchestra are also excellent, performing at tempos that seem natural and unhurried, the opposite of some of the other period-instrument versions available. The recording is spacious but clear, almost recreating the ambience of a church.

■

J.S. BACH: *The St. Matthew Passion*
La Chapelle Royale, Collegium Vocale of Ghent/
    Philippe Herreweghe
Harmonia Mundi   HMX 2901155.57

JOHANN SEBASTIAN BACH (1685–1750):
The Mass in B Minor

There have always been questions and confusion about the reasons behind the composition of the Mass in B Minor by J.S. Bach. Why would a Lutheran church composer in Leipzig write a high Roman Catholic Mass? But to Bach, music was a hobby as well as a vocation. He was a scholar of music as well as a composer. He pored over the scores of the old masters who preceded him and was very knowledgeable about their styles, techniques, methods, and talents. He was also very aware of what and how his contemporaries across Europe were composing. As he grew older, Bach became more and more interested in leaving examples of his musical art to the future. *The Art of Fugue* is one obvious example, but the B Minor Mass is another. It's a kind of sourcebook of the state of mass composition at the midpoint of the eighteenth century – a specimen book or a how-to guide. Many great composers before Bach had composed masses, and it's not surprising that Bach himself wanted to try his hand at it and make his own contribution to the great legacy and tradition of the musical mass. He never heard the work performed during his lifetime, and he may have never intended it to be performed as a whole. Lutheran masses contain only the first two sections, the Kyrie and Gloria. And the overall length of the B Minor Mass made it unsuitable for both Catholic and Lutheran services.

Bach created the B Minor Mass in a piecemeal fashion over a period of about twenty-five years, between 1724 and 1749. Much of it was culled and reworked from previous music he had composed. So it is a wonder how concise and well-designed the work is. It's very unified, as if he wrote the mass in one sitting. Throughout his life, Bach was always on the lookout to improve his status as a composer, and in 1733 he sent the Kyrie and Gloria sections of the mass to the new Elector of Saxony in Dresden. Three years later, Bach received a new title from the Elector, and was able to fulfill its requirements while maintaining his job in Leipzig, with only occasional trips to Dresden.

With his love and knowledge of musical styles and techniques, old and new, Bach employed a mixture of styles and techniques in the B Minor Mass. There are sections that clearly show the influence of earlier music from the Renaissance, from nationalities as diverse as German, Italian, and Flemish, using a variety of musical forms, including the operatic aria. The Mass is the crowning peak of Bach's sacred music, and one of the greatest musical creations of all time. His use of his faith as a powerful inspiration is perhaps nowhere better shown. The early nineteenth-century Swiss music critic Hans Georg Nägeli called it, "the greatest work of music of all ages and of all peoples."

For decades, large choirs and orchestras performed the B Minor Mass, often compromising clarity and articulation, for grandeur and impact. In more recent years, the practice of one-to-a-part has sprung up. John Eliot Gardiner's recording takes the best of both worlds. The excellent Monteverdi Choir is a force of only about twenty-five singers, and the vocal solos are taken by choir members. The result is a clear, light texture but without any loss of the weight and depth needed for the work to come across successfully. Gardiner never loses sight of the overall structure and impact of the mass. At times, as in the Gloria section, the performances are thrilling, while at other times, there's a quiet and proud devotion. It's a work and a recording that will never tire, even after years of repeated listenings.

J.S. BACH: *The Mass in B Minor*
The Monteverdi Choir & The English Baroque Soloists/
   John Eliot Gardiner
Archiv 415 514-2

George Frideric Handel (1685–1759): *Messiah*

Without question, the oratorio *Messiah* by George Frideric Handel is the most frequently performed work for choir and orchestra in the entire classical music repertoire. And *Messiah* has held that exalted position for more than 260 years. Today, the work is usually heard in the weeks leading up to Christmas in concert halls and churches in English-speaking countries around the world. But during his lifetime, Handel always performed the work in the spring, during the Easter season. The premiere took place in Dublin in April 1742. The oratorio does make more sense linked to the Easter season, than to Christmas. Part I of *Messiah* deals with the prophecy of God to redeem us by the arrival of a Messiah, and the story of the birth of Christ. But after that, the focus of the work shifts to Christ's sacrifice. Part II is the story of redemption, our rejection of God's offer, and eventual defeat. And Part III is our thanksgiving for the final defeat of death itself, and our happiness at the prospect of eternal life.

Handel turned to the form of oratorio in the 1730s, after London audiences cooled to the Italian operas he had been composing. Most of his oratorios were based on stories from the Old Testament and themes from Jewish history: Deborah, Saul, Israel in Egypt, Samson, and Solomon. But the text of *Messiah* was taken largely from the New Testament, compiled by Handel's friend and admirer, the amateur poet Charles Jennens. It is interesting to note that the title of the work uses the Old Testament Hebrew term "Messiah," instead of the New Testament Greek equivalent, "Christ."

38 ·

Handel composed the oratorio in a burst of creative energy over a period of a little less than a month in the summer of 1741. During the composition, he admitted to a friend, "I did think I saw all Heaven before me, and the great God himself." The profits from the first performance went to charity, and there was such a demand for tickets that the organizers publicly requested that the ladies not wear hooped skirts, and that the gentlemen not carry their swords at the performance.

Regardless of how it is performed today, whether authentically with a choir of twenty-five or thirty, or grandly with a choir of two hundred, *Messiah* continues to reach out and hold audiences in a way few other choral works do. Maybe it's because of Handel's brilliant, theatrical, almost operatic way of telling the familiar story. Maybe it's because of the warm and expressive quality of the arias and choruses. Or maybe it's just because of the wealth of great melodies. Whatever the reason, *Messiah* will undoubtedly continue to enthrall us, enjoying a worldwide popularity like no other work.

John Eliot Gardiner picks up on the theatrical sense of Handel and produces a *Messiah* that is high on drama. But he doesn't ignore the mystery and awe of the work, and some of the choruses, like the end of "All We Like Sheep," have a powerful impact. The Monteverdi Choir and the orchestra, the English Baroque Soloists, are both exceptional, as is the cast of soloists. Typical of Gardiner, tempos here are quick and textures light, but the results are bouncing rhythms and clean articulation. This is an authoritative, highly musical, and satisfying account.

■

GEORGE FRIDERIC HANDEL: *Messiah*
The Monteverdi Choir and the English Baroque Soloists/
   John Eliot Gardiner
Philips   434 297-2

GEORGE FRIDERIC HANDEL (1685–1759):
Water Music

The Thames River has always been an important English water-way. For centuries, it was the major thoroughfare for commerce and goods in and out of England. But in the seventeenth and eighteenth centuries, it was also an important social vehicle for English royalty, who used the river as a way to see and be seen by their loyal subjects.

It's believed that the "Water Music" by Handel was the result of one such royal excursion. The story goes that in the summer of 1717, King George I, who usually avoided public appearances, planned a lavish journey one evening on barges up the Thames River, from Whitehall to Chelsea. After dinner in Chelsea, in the wee hours of the morning, the flotilla then returned to St. James's Palace. According to eyewitness accounts, the English came out in droves to see their royalty, and the number of boats on the Thames was "beyond counting." During the trip, the King and his courtiers were entertained by music by Handel, performed in an open barge that travelled parallel to the royal barge.

A contemporary London newspaper report described the affair: "Many other barges with persons of quality attended, and so great a number of boats that the whole river in a manner was covered. A City Company's barge was employed for the music, wherein were fifty instruments of all sorts, who played the finest symphonies, composed express for this occasion by Mr. Handel, which his majesty liked so well that he caused it to be played over three times in going and returning."

The symphonies referred to in the newspaper account were really a group of orchestral suites by Handel that have come to be known collectively as the "Water Music." Handel was one of the great businessmen in music – a composer who seemed to know exactly what was needed for each occasion he composed for, and how to achieve it. For this royal barge excursion, he mostly composed open-air music that employed the brilliance of horns, trumpets, and drums. But one of the suites featured some of the more gentle instruments – the flute, recorder, oboe, bassoon, and strings. It's believed that this music, of a more intimate nature, was played during the late-night meal in Chelsea. The "Water Music" is a collection of very tuneful music that exudes courtly elegance and grace, as well as pomp and majesty. It's extroverted music, suitable for royalty, but, as it was in 1717, easily enjoyed by the masses as well.

Tafelmusik, on period instruments, under director Jeanne Lamon gives a very successful, lively reading of the "Water Music," that combines majesty and grace with warmth and musicality. Instead of presenting the suites separately, they provide a combined version, with the movements of the two brass suites woven together, in the belief that Handel might have done this for concert performances. Long gone are the days when this music was heard outdoors and Tafelmusik seems to rightly downplay that aspect. The tempos are just right, and the excellent playing, especially by the winds and brass, provides the perfect mix – an essential extroverted quality without any blatty harshness.

■ ———————————————————————

GEORGE FRIDERIC HANDEL: *Water Music*
Tafelmusik/Jeanne Lamon
Sony Classical   SK 68257

GEORGE FRIDERIC HANDEL (1685–1759):
Music for the Royal Fireworks

Thirty years after the "Water Music," Handel composed music for another royal occasion, which has become almost as popular. In 1748, the Treaty of Aix-La-Chapelle ended the War of the Austrian Succession. England had entered this war reluctantly and gained little from the spoils. But nevertheless, King George II felt that there should be some kind of public celebration and a spectacular fireworks event was planned for London's Green Park. A huge wooden structure was built along the lines of an ancient Greek temple, complete with columns, statues of Greek gods, and a sculpture of King George himself. Handel was asked by the king to write suitable music, but there were some conditions. In his desire to make the commemorative event militaristic, the king specified that there should only be martial instruments used, and "no fiddles." Handel must have been shocked by this royal command, but who was he to argue with the King of England? He scored the music for nine trumpets, nine horns, twenty-four oboes, twelve bassoons (including contrabassoon), several pairs of kettledrums, and a variety of other military drums. He subsequently added string parts, and doubled the oboes and bassoons for a concert performance of the work a month later.

The evening of fireworks finally arrived, but it quickly turned into disaster. Many of the fireworks failed to ignite, while some went off at the wrong times. And eventually, part of the wooden Greek temple caught fire and burned to the ground. The designer of the event became so enraged that he drew his sword on the man responsible for the fireworks and had to be taken into custody.

How much of Handel's music was actually heard in the ensuing pandemonium, and its effect on the public, can only be guessed. But today, the "Music for the Royal Fireworks" by Handel, with or without strings, is loved for its entertaining, jubilant, and triumphant qualities. The glories and romance of war may be rightly frowned upon today, but not this glorious music.

The Four Coronation Anthems by Handel, also included on this recording, were composed for the coronation of King George II in Westminster Abbey in 1727. Zadok the Priest is probably the most popular, mainly for its highly effective stately orchestral opening, which slowly builds until the glorious first entry of the choir. It has been used at every British coronation since 1727.

Today, you usually hear the "Music for the Royal Fireworks" performed with strings. But in his Hyperion recording, Robert King uses period instruments in Handel's original scoring for winds, brass, and percussion only. This original version offers a glimpse into the extravagance and exuberance planned for the first performance in London in 1729. The blend of all the oboes, bassoons, trumpets, horns, and drums produces a glorious, rich sound. The recordings of both the "Music for the Royal Fireworks" and the Coronation Anthems are spacious and roomy. They work very well in capturing the regal ambience of a British coronation in Westminster Abbey.

■ ───────────────────────────────────

GEORGE FRIDERIC HANDEL: *Music for the Royal Fireworks,*
   Coronation Anthems
The King's Consort/Robert King
Hyperion   CDA 20350

FRANZ JOSEPH HAYDN (1732–1809):
String Quartets Op. 76, Nos. 4, 5, 6

Joseph Haydn is often called "Papa" Haydn in part because of his compassionate and caring way with the musicians under him at his job at the Eszterháza court, then in Austria. But another, more important reason, is the marked development that Haydn made in the forms of the symphony, sonata, and string quartet. He enlarged them, refined and consolidated their structures, and experimented with textures, harmonies, and sonorities. And in so doing, Haydn established them as concise musical works, which enhanced their musical expression and inspired later composers to continue their development. Although he didn't invent any of them, the advances to the symphony, sonata, and string quartet achieved by Haydn were so important that he is sometimes considered to have "fathered" them.

The great German Romantic writer Goethe described the string quartet this way: "You listen to four sensible persons conversing, you profit from their discourse, and you get to know the peculiar properties of their instruments."

When Haydn began writing his more than eighty string quartets, the instrumental makeup had become established as two violins, viola, and cello. His most famous quartets are the six that make up his Op. 76, composed after his second very successful trip to London. By the time he returned to Vienna in 1795, he was regarded as one of the most talented and popular composers in Europe, and he knew it. He was in his mid-sixties, with over thirty years of experience in writing music for the string quartet. As a result, the Op. 76 quartets have a certain confidence and self-assurance to them, composed by a man at the peak of his creative powers. They are strong and bold, with more emotional slow movements, faster and wittier minuets, and more complex finales than his earlier compositions. The String Quartet Op. 76, No. 4 by Haydn has the nickname "Sunrise" because of the opening, where the first violin climbs slowly over a sustained chord, suggesting the morning sun slowly rising above the horizon. In Op. 76, No. 5, the slow second movement is almost as long as the other three movements combined. It's one of Haydn's finest and a good example of the emotional intensity that Haydn inserted into the second movements of all six quartets. The last of the set, Op. 76, No. 6, as well as having an emotionally charged second movement, also contains a lively finale whose offbeat accents and harmonies must have sounded quite modern at the time.

The Kodaly Quartet has recorded the complete string quartets by Haydn for the Naxos label, and it is an amazingly consistent set over the eighty quartets. A rich, blended, and balanced string sound, elegant, refined and shapely phrasing and commitment make it obvious that the Kodaly Quartet loves this music. Throughout this Naxos set, there is a vitality and freshness to every quartet, as if it were being played for the first time. The budget price of this recording makes it all the more worth buying.

■──

FRANZ JOSEPH HAYDN: *String Quartets, Op. 76, Nos. 4, 5, 6*
The Kodaly Quartet
Naxos 8.550315

~

FRANZ JOSEPH HAYDN (1732–1809):
Symphonies Nos. 85, 86, 87

During his thirty years of service to the Esterházy family at the court of Eszterháza, Haydn's responsibilities left him little time for travelling. He was just too busy to hock and promote his musical wares. But in 1779, Haydn signed a contract with the Esterházys that permitted him to accept outside work from others, and with advances in printing and publishing, his music quickly became known all over Europe. One of the countries that grew to adore his compositions was France. So much so, that music by less accomplished composers was often pirated and printed in France under Haydn's name.

In 1784, Haydn received a commission to compose six symphonies for a Paris concert organization called Le Concert de la Loge Olympique that had links to the liberal-thinking Freemasons, to which Haydn and Mozart both belonged. The orchestra of the Loge Olympique performed in long sky-blue coats and lace ruffles, with swords hanging from their belts. Haydn's stature at the time was such that the Loge offered him five times what they normally offered a composer for a commission, and the fee was further upped for the publication rights. It was one of the best-paying commissions Haydn was ever to receive.

Haydn composed the set of six symphonies, Nos. 82 through 87, between 1785 and 1786, and they have suitably come to be known as the "Paris" Symphonies. Parisian audiences of the late eighteenth century loved them. One contemporary Paris review described Haydn as, "quite the opposite of those sterile composers who pass continually from one idea to another instead of choosing a single, variable one; and who produce mechanically one effect after another, without linking them, and without taste." The six symphonies became so popular that nicknames began to be attached to some of them. The No. 82 soon became "L'Ours" or "The Bear," because of the finale that suggested music that might accompany a dancing bear. The No. 83 was tagged "La Poule" or "The Hen" because of the repeated clucking figure of the oboe in the first movement. And the No. 85 was called "La Reine" or "The Queen" because it was the favourite of Queen Marie Antoinette. Unfortunately, the Queen wasn't able to enjoy it for long. She was beheaded in 1793.

In the 1990s, Tafelmusik, with director Jeanne Lamon and conductor Bruno Weil, had planned to record the complete 104 Haydn Symphonies for Sony Classical. Like several others before them, the group wasn't able to complete the daunting project, but luckily, the six Paris symphonies did get recorded. Performing on period instruments with a perfect balance between strings, winds, and brass, Tafelmusik achieves a clarity and articulation that allows Haydn's high spirits, wit, and character to come across beautifully. Tafelmusik has rarely played as well as on this record. And their high standards, energy, and vitality only make it all the more regrettable that the full 104 symphonies were not recorded.

■ ————————————————————————————————

FRANZ JOSEPH HAYDN: *Symphonies Nos. 85, 86, 87*
Tafelmusik/Bruno Weil
Sony Classical   SK 66296

FRANZ JOSEPH HAYDN (1732–1809):
Die Schöpfung (The Creation)

After thirty years of service to the Eszterháza court, Haydn twice visited London in 1791–92 and 1794–95. His music was performed there, and he was wined and dined by the nobility and generally fawned over. At one point, Haydn attended a festival of music by George Frideric Handel, the late Baroque master, who had been based in London. Although he had heard the music before, Haydn was so impressed by the performance, especially of the oratorios, that he began to think of composing an oratorio himself – a musical field to which he had not yet contributed. Haydn was presented with a libretto, based on the story of the creation of the world as described in *Paradise Lost* by the seventeenth-century English poet John Milton, and in Genesis. He sketched out some ideas immediately, but on his return to Vienna in 1795, Haydn gave the text to Baron Gottfried van Swieten, the court librarian. Van Swieten was a prominent man in Vienna. As well as being the librarian, he was also a writer, poet, translator, composer, and a devoted patron of the arts. Haydn asked van Swieten to shorten the text, translate it from English into German, and to suggest some musical treatments of it. Van Swieten did all three, and Haydn began to compose *The Creation* in 1796. It was a labour of love, and he struggled over the composition. At one point he wrote, "I have never felt so devout as when I was working on *The Creation*. Every day I fell on my knees and prayed to God to give me the strength to finish the work successfully." *The Creation* was premiered to acclaim in Vienna in 1798, and was quickly taken up across Europe.

Haydn actually made two versions of the oratorio – one in German, one in English – each with slightly different melodic lines to fit the inflections, stresses, and rhythms of the two languages. Today, both versions are performed. When sung in German, the work tends to be known as *Die Schöpfung*. In English, it's *The Creation*.

The oratorio is divided into three parts. Part I deals with the first four days of the earth's creation. Part II represents the fifth and sixth days, and the appearance of plant and animal life. And Part III deals with the seventh day and the early, blissful existence of Adam and Eve.

The opening orchestral introduction, called "The Representation of Chaos," is one of the most famous in all music. Haydn paints the dark, frightening void prior to Creation through snippets of melody, vague rhythms, strange harmonies, awkward dissonances, and sudden outbursts. Then, to depict the creation of light, Haydn has a blaze of music breaking the darkness with the musical equivalent of blinding sunlight.

Haydn's *The Creation* was composed at a time when just about everyone was what we now call a creationist, and before advances in science had presented a reasonable alternative to the biblical explanation of our roots. And today, the work is sometimes criticized for its naive view of the world. Haydn was content to present a work that simply depicted the awesome wonders of God. His genius comes out in how he drew them. Encouraged by Baron van Swieten, Haydn used quite a bit of word-painting in *The Creation*, a compositional technique where the meaning of the words is enhanced by their musical representation. An example would be the use of a harsh dissonance on the word "pain." Haydn had a great theatrical sense and the ability to colour and animate subjects in music, and in no work is this more evident than in *The Creation*.

It's the theatrical sense of conductor John Eliot Gardiner that makes his recording of Haydn's *Die Schöpfung* (in German) so highly regarded. Gardiner seems to be able to balance the mystery and awestruck qualities of the work, with fun, humour, and celebration. The soloists, choir, and orchestra are all impeccably disciplined with clear entries and confident enthusiasm, nicely captured by the warm recording.

■───

FRANZ JOSEPH HAYDN: *Die Schöpfung (The Creation)*
The Monteverdi Choir & The English Baroque Soloists/
    John Eliot Gardiner
Archiv   449 217-2

WOLFGANG AMADEUS MOZART (1756–1791):
Symphony No. 38, K. 504, "Prague"

Mozart composed his first symphonies in the 1760s before the age of ten. For the most part, they were well-crafted and effective. But they were imitations of contemporary symphonies by the likes of Johann Christian Bach, and Mozart's father, Leopold, had provided a helping hand. By the time he penned the Symphony No. 29 in the 1770s, Mozart's style had developed and started to congeal. He had heard and absorbed the works of his contemporaries, like Haydn, incorporated their styles into his own, and showed the maturity and craft of the master. By the time of the last few symphonies in the late 1780s, Mozart had further developed his own unique style, and these final few works can easily be included in a list of the greatest symphonies ever composed.

Vienna never really embraced Mozart with open arms, and the city's fickle music lovers began to cool to him by the mid-1780s, finding his music too involved and complex to be entertaining. In 1786, the opera *The Marriage of Figaro* had premiered in Vienna, but despite good audiences, it closed after only a few performances, largely for political reasons. The city of Prague decided to take it on, and invited Mozart to attend some of the performances early in 1787. By the time Mozart arrived in Prague in mid-January, 1787, Prague was *Figaro*-crazy. Arrangements of arias from the opera were being performed in the city's salons and coffee houses, and turned into dances for its ballrooms. Mozart said, "My Prague people understand me." While he was in Prague Mozart's latest symphony was also performed. It's come to be known as the "Prague Symphony" – a work with three movements, instead of the usual four. It's believed that Prague music lovers at the time were still more familiar and comfortable with the three movement symphony, and Mozart, eager to please, was pandering to Czech tastes. After a month of successes, rare in his lifetime, Mozart returned home to Vienna, with a commission for a new opera. *Don Giovanni* was premiered in Prague later that year and, once again, took the city by storm.

As well as the three-movement form, another aspect of the "Prague" Symphony by Mozart that stands out is the slow introduction to the first movement. This was more common in Haydn's music, but not in Mozart's. Only three symphonies by Mozart begin with an introduction. (One of the others is the Symphony No. 36, K. 425, "Linz," also included on this recording.)

It's the last three symphonies by Mozart – Nos. 39, 40, and 41 – that are usually regarded as the culmination of his symphonic output, all composed during the summer of 1788. But for skill, quality, and verve, the Symphony No. 38, "Prague," should be included in that esteemed company.

It may seem that I'm trying to forcibly link a recording of the "Prague" Symphony by Mozart with a contemporary Prague orchestra. But the complete Telarc set of the Mozart symphonies with conductor Sir Charles Mackerras and the Prague Chamber Orchestra is excellent, and that's the reason I'm recommending this recording. Although the orchestra plays on conventional, not period instruments, Mackerras brings an authentic approach to the performance, nevertheless. A harpsichord is included, and first and second violins are split, left and right, heightening the dialogues that exist in the music. These performances may lack a bit in elegance and grace, but they easily make up for it in heart and soul.

■ ———————————————————————————————————

W.A. MOZART: *Symphony No. 38, K. 504, "Prague"*
Prague Chamber Orchestra/Sir Charles Mackerras
Telarc   CD-80148

WOLFGANG AMADEUS MOZART (1756–1791): *Piano Concertos Nos. 15, 21, 23*

During the Baroque period the solo concerto had evolved from the Concerto grosso form, but it really came of age at the end of the Classical period. And Mozart was one of its most important composers. As a brilliant violinist and pianist, Mozart moulded the concerto to suit his own needs and goals. After he made the break from his hometown of Salzburg in 1781 and moved permanently to Vienna, Mozart enjoyed moderate success as a pianist and teacher. He composed many piano concertos in the early 1780s for use as vehicles at his own concerts. The Viennese audiences enjoyed the showmanship of performers, but Mozart was too good a composer to offer them only flash and bravura. He knew that he had to strike a balance between artistry and virtuosity.

Mozart's popularity in Vienna reached its peak in 1784–85. At one point, he wrote to his father in Salzburg that he had performed a total of twenty-two concerts in thirty-eight days. Not surprisingly, he added, "I don't think that in this way I can possibly get out of practice."

The Piano Concerto in B-flat, K. 450 was one of several he composed for his own use in Vienna in 1784. It exhibits Mozart's new level of compositional ability and keyboard virtuosity and many pianists regard it as one of Mozart's most difficult. In a letter to his father, Mozart described it as one that "makes the performer sweat."

He composed the Piano Concerto in C, K. 467 a year later. This one carries the nickname "Elvira Madigan." In recent years, some have believed that Elvira Madigan was a love interest of Mozart's, or the dedicatee, or even a pianist who made a famous recording of this work. In fact, the nickname has nothing to do with Mozart. *Elvira Madigan* was the title of a 1960s Swedish art film, in which the slow second movement of this concerto was used at length throughout. Today, the huge popularity of this movement on its own makes it difficult for us to listen to it with fresh ears. But the piano sings throughout the movement, gently accompanied by the orchestra. The Mozart scholar Alfred Einstein maybe described it best when he said "[It is] an ideal aria freed from the limitations of the human voice."

Like the Piano Concerto in B-flat, K. 450, the Concerto in A, K. 488 was composed for Mozart's own use during the season of Lent, when the theatres and opera houses of Vienna were closed. K. 488 was first heard during Lent in 1786, and, on the surface at least, this concerto carries the cheery character of the opera *The Marriage of Figaro*, first performed in Vienna a little later the same year, after the opera houses had reopened. But this concerto has a darker side too. Underneath the light exterior are deeper emotions of melancholy, especially in the second movement. For the finale, Mozart pushes aside any feelings of doom and gloom, and the concerto ends optimistically.

Pianist Alfred Brendel brings solid musicianship and refinement to his recordings of the Mozart concertos. Everything has been planned and rehearsed beforehand, and yet these still have great life, spontaneity, and freshness. Brendel is matched every step of the way by the Academy of St. Martin-in-the-Fields, and Neville Marriner, who offer great support, good teamwork, and a sympathetic approach.

■ _____

W.A. MOZART: *Piano Concertos Nos. 15, 21, 23*
Alfred Brendel, The Academy of St. Martin-in-the-Fields/
    Sir Neville Marriner
Philips 464 719-2

WOLFGANG AMADEUS MOZART (1756–1791): *Requiem, K. 626*

The story of the composition of the *Requiem* by Mozart has always been popular, and never more than today. The fictionalized versions of the story in the play *Amadeus* by Peter Schaffer and the subsequent Academy-award winning film by Milos Forman have lent the tale legendary status.

In the last year of his life, Mozart received a commission from a stranger for a requiem mass. The fee offered was substantial. Half of it would be paid up front and the other half on completion. Given his financial situation at the time, Mozart was in no position to refuse. He accepted the terms and set to work. There have been many romantic accounts of how Mozart believed that the stranger was the Grim Reaper himself, and that he was writing his own requiem. This fancy arose after Mozart's death. His work on other projects, such as the operas *Die Zauberflöte* (*The Magic Flute*) and *La Clemenza di Tito* (*The Clemency of Titus*), delayed him, and he died before finishing the score of the *Requiem*. He had completed the opening Introit and Kyrie sections, sketched out parts of the rest, but never reached the end. His widow, Constanze, pregnant and with debts mounting, was reluctant to return the first half of the commission fee, and approached several musicians to complete what Mozart had begun. They all turned her down. She then called on one of Mozart's students, Franz Xaver Süssmayr who had discussed the work with Mozart on his deathbed. Constanze was able to give Süssmayr the remaining sketches and fragments of the requiem. He completed the composition, Constanze received the balance of the commission fee, and for two hundred years, the

Süssmayr completion of the Mozart Requiem was the one used. But there's always been the question of how much of the *Requiem* was Mozart's, and how much was Süssmayr's. In recent years, the Süssmayr version has come under criticism and several musicologists have tried their hands at revision and completion, based on their own research. Of these newer completions, the most popular is by Robert Levin, an American pianist and musicologist, and it's Levin's version that was used for this recording.

The differences from the Süssmayr version are not overly pronounced, as Levin wisely saw his goal as being "to revise not as much, but as little as possible." Süssmayr did have the advantage of knowing Mozart and discussing the score of the requiem with him. Keeping this in mind, Levin observed, as he says, "the character, texture, voice leading, continuity and structure of Mozart's music," and "retained the traditional version insofar as it agrees with idiomatic Mozartean practice."

The *Requiem* demonstrates Mozart's brilliance in combining the gravity of church music with the drama of opera. In his style and approach, he was decades ahead of his time. The *Requiem* is a Romantic work that deals with the awe and mystery of life and death. Maybe Beethoven said it best when he purportedly remarked, "If Mozart did not write the music, then the man who wrote it was a Mozart."

This recording was made live in upstate New York two weeks after the tragedies of September 11, 2001. Maybe that's why there seems to be a spirituality and concentration here that can't be ignored. Bernard Labadie and his Canadian musicians provide a gripping account, with crisp diction and clean articulation from soloists, choir, and orchestra.

■ ───

W.A. MOZART: *Requiem, K. 626 (Robert Levin version)*
La Chapelle du Quebec, Les Violons du Roy/Bernard Labadie
Dorian DOR-90310

WOLFGANG AMADEUS MOZART (1756–1791):
Operatic & Sacred Music Selections

Few would argue that Mozart was one of the greatest musical geniuses of all time. In his short life, he composed more than six hundred works in all the major forms: symphonies, concertos, sonatas, songs, chamber music, church music, and operas. And all of them show his astonishing mastery of the form – there really isn't a weak work in his output. But his true genius manifests itself best in his vocal music – the operas and sacred music. Many believe that Mozart was primarily a great composer of song, and that his instrumental and orchestral music were merely vocal music in disguise.

But what really inspired Mozart was characterization. To him, music was drama and theatre, it was about relationships, emotions, and perspectives – whether between characters on the opera stage, or between a soloist and the orchestra in a concerto. In his operas, Mozart created living, breathing, realistic people. Some of his operas were serious, some comic, and some, like *Don Giovanni*, contained elements of both. The opera stage seems to dissolve as the characters and their circumstances develop into enlightening stories about personalities, points of view, and the interplay between them. The music covers a huge range of emotions and moods – from tenderness to humour, from mockery and irony to anger and revenge, and jealousy to forgiveness. By their concentration on his characters, Mozart's operas have a tight structure, both musically and dramatically. Few others in the history of music have had these skills to this extent.

Mozart's gift for characterization can also be seen in his sacred music. Faith, devotion, thanksgiving, praise, and prayer now take the place of jealousy, rage, revenge, and humour. But the human emotions conveyed again drive the music. There are parts of the *Requiem* that could have easily been borrowed from one of his Italian operas, such as *The Marriage of Figaro* or *Così Fan Tutte*. To Mozart, music was music, regardless of conventions and genres.

In 1906, the sequicentenary of Mozart's birth, the great pianist, composer, and conductor Ferruccio Busoni came out with a series of observations on Mozart, one for each year of Mozart's life. Here are a few that sum him up nicely.

He has light and shade at his command, but his light never blinds and his darkness does not obscure a clear outline.

In the most tragic situations he has a joke ready, in comic ones he can be serious.

In his versatility he is universal.

His smile is not a diplomat's smile, nor an actor's; it is the smile of a pure spirit – and yet of a man of the world.

He is the perfect and rounded figure, the sum total, an end and not a beginning.

He is as young as a boy, as wise as an old man; never out of date, never modern; he has gone to his grave yet is still alive.

His smile, that was so human, is transfigured and shines on us still.

The recommended recording is a strong two-disc compilation set of highlights from Mozart's operas and sacred music. There are selections from *The Marriage of Figaro*, *Don Giovanni*, *The Magic Flute* and others, as well as the Mass in C Minor, the Vespers, K. 339, and a few songs. The performers include Cecilia Bartoli, Bryn Terfel, Kathleen Battle, Emma Kirkby, Stuart Burrows, Kiri Te Kanawa among others, conducted by such talents as Sir Colin

Davis, Sir Neville Marriner, Christopher Hogwood, and Sir Georg Solti.

■ ────────────────────────────────────

W.A. MOZART: *The Voice of Mozart – Operatic & Sacred Music Selections*
A variety of singers, ensembles and conductors
Decca   289 470 505-2

WOLFGANG AMADEUS MOZART (1756–1791):
String Quartet in C, K. 465, "Dissonance"

Like all of the great composers, Mozart absorbed what was happening in the styles and approaches of music around him, moulded them to his own fashion, and incorporated them into his compositions.

Mozart had written string quartets in his youth that showed a certain amount of skill, but there's a huge leap in quality between the early quartets and those he composed in the 1780s in Vienna. By that time, Mozart had met and befriended Haydn and had come to know some of the string quartets by his elder contemporary. The effect was huge, and Mozart's quartet-writing moved into full maturity. He gave all four instruments equal treatment, created more varieties of texture, and made better use of counterpoint, or the conversational aspect of the four instruments together.

Between 1782 and 1785, Mozart composed a set of six string quartets, dedicating them to Haydn, from whom he had learned so much. They've come to be known by the somewhat confusing title of the "Haydn" Quartets by Mozart. In the dedication to Haydn, Mozart wrote, "I send my six sons to you, most celebrated and very dear friend. They are, indeed, the fruit of a long and arduous labour; but the hope that many friends have given me that this toil will be in some degree rewarded, encourages me and flatters me with the thought that these children may one day be a source of consolation to me."

As Mozart mentions, he found the composition of these six quartets difficult, and in the manuscripts, his effort is clearly shown by the many crossings-out, erasures, changes, and alterations he made – unusual for Mozart. It's believed that the six quartets were premiered in Vienna in 1785. Both Haydn and Mozart's father, Leopold, were present. Mozart himself is believed to have played viola. The comments made by Haydn to Leopold Mozart afterward have become the stuff of legend. Pulling Mozart's father aside, Haydn purportedly said, "I say to you before God and as an honest man that your son is the greatest composer known to me, either in person or by reputation. He has taste and, what is more, the greatest knowledge of the technique of composition." This was high praise from one of Europe's most popular and highly regarded composers at the time.

The String Quartet in C, K. 465, is the last of the six "Haydn" Quartets. Its nickname "Dissonance" comes from the opening slow introduction. In it, Mozart creates such a high degree of tension in the melody and harmony that it must have been a shock to its early audiences. It is dark and dissonant, leading many at the time to conclude that the notes had been printed incorrectly. But Mozart contrasts the slow introduction in the movement proper, which is more conventional and has a bright, radiant character.

This recording is Volume 4 of the complete string quartets by Mozart recorded by the Eder Quartet for the budget-priced Naxos label. The entire series is strong, but this particular recording is one of the finest. The Eder Quartet has a warm, balanced, and blended sound and a wonderful sense of Mozart's style. The spacious recorded sound has a nice bloom, without losing any presence or clarity.

■ ─────────────────────────────────────

W.A. MOZART: *String Quartet in C, K. 465, "Dissonance"*
The Eder Quartet
Naxos 8.550543

LUDWIG VAN BEETHOVEN (1770–1827): *Symphonies Nos. 5 & 7*

Few composers achieved as much as Beethoven did in expanding the scope and importance of the symphony. He made the instrumentation larger and richer, his movements were longer and were linked, and his treatment of the musical material was more complex. In essence, the symphony in Beethoven's hands was less of a form of entertainment, and more of a personal expression of ideals and concepts. Although he had, as he said, "struck out on a new path" with his Symphony No. 3, it's the famous Symphony No. 5 that best illustrates these objectives. Here, Beethoven tossed aside many of the eighteenth-century classical symphonic formalities and traits and he gave more importance and weight to the final movement than to the opening movement.

The Beethoven Fifth represents a struggle with some kind of oppressor – an enemy, or destiny, or fate. The opening theme, sometimes called the "Fate" theme, contains the most famous four notes in history, and dominates the movement (ta-ta-ta-TAH). It's not surprising that in the Second World War, the Allies used this theme as a symbol for Victory. (Three short dashes, followed by one long one represents the letter V in Morse code.) But, by the arrival of the finale in a blaze of glory, we have overcome the oppressor and we emerge triumphant. The approach is also sometimes described as a journey from darkness into light, and it was a symphonic style that many composers after Beethoven continued – from Brahms to Mahler, even Shostakovich.

Richard Wagner described the Symphony No. 7 by Beethoven as "the apotheosis of the dance. Tables and benches, cans and cups, the grandmother, the blind and the lame, the children in the cradle, all fall to dancing."

Wagner wasn't suggesting that we should dance to the symphony. He was commenting on its rhythmical strength and the powerful momentum and force, where you can't help but tap your foot or finger. By the finale, the entire orchestra seems to be galloping headstrong together in one of Beethoven's most powerful cries for freedom.

The late conductor Carlos Kleiber has always been a bit of an enigma – he avoided permanent positions and rarely recorded. But when he did make a recording, it was usually because he had something important to say, and it often became a classic. These recordings of the Beethoven Symphonies Nos. 5 and 7 have been highly regarded ever since their original release in the 1970s. Tempos are often on the fast side, but Kleiber shows he's a master of control and pacing, and he keeps the big picture always in mind. The performances of both works give you the sense that the musicians are playing this music for the very first time, and that we are hearing it for the first time. There's a driven, powerful force to them that is infectious, while the slow movements are pictures of restraint, without ever touching on the sentimental.

■ ————————————————————————

LUDWIG VAN BEETHOVEN: *Symphonies Nos. 5 and 7*
Vienna Philharmonic Orchestra/Carlos Kleiber
DGG   447 400-2

LUDWIG VAN BEETHOVEN (1770–1827):
Piano Concerto No. 5 in E-flat Major, Op. 73, "Emperor"

By the time Beethoven completed his last piano concerto, the No. 5, he was almost totally deaf. He had composed the previous four piano concertos with himself in mind as the soloist, but by the time of the No. 5, the "Emperor," his hearing was so far gone, he realized it was too risky for him to be the soloist.

Much of the "Emperor" Concerto was composed during Napoleon's siege of Vienna in 1809. There are stories of Beethoven hiding in basements holding pillows to his ears, trying to save the last vestiges of his hearing from the bomb blasts. The origin of the nickname "Emperor" is not clear, but there is a story that, at the Vienna premiere, one of the officers of the occupying French army was heard to comment, "C'est l'Empereur!" The nickname seemed to suggest many of the qualities of the concerto, and it's been attached ever since. Beethoven, who was not a fan of Napoleon's, would probably have been disgusted with it.

When Beethoven first arrived in Vienna from his hometown of Bonn in 1792, he made his mark as a brilliant pianist. His reputation as a great composer came later. In his first three piano concertos, he strove to show the pianist's command of the instrument. In the No. 4, he began to focus more on the music's expressive qualities. By the time of No. 5, he was pushing the limited range of the pianos used in Vienna at the time, as well as the conventions of the eighteenth-century classical concerto. In the "Emperor," Beethoven created a work that is less of a dialogue between piano and orchestra and more of a depiction of a dramatic struggle, eventually resulting in victory. Through the three movements, there is a wonderful combination of the heroic, the poetic, and the joyful. Both his Symphony No. 3, nicknamed the "Eroica," and the Piano Concerto No. 5, "Emperor," are in the key of E-flat, a key that Beethoven often used to suggest majesty, nobility, and grandeur.

The Austrian-born American pianist Rudolf Serkin was one of the great Beethoven pianists of the twentieth century, and in this recording he was perfectly matched with the New York Philharmonic Orchestra under its music director at the time, Leonard Bernstein. Both Serkin and Bernstein approach the work with the majestic pride so crucial to the success of the piece. But they also bring to it, especially in the Rondo Finale, a sense of fun and friendship – sheer joy at making great music together. It's an approach that Beethoven himself used to refer to as "unbuttoned."

■ _____

LUDWIG VAN BEETHOVEN: *Piano Concerto No. 5 in E-flat Major,*
   Op. 73, "Emperor"
Rudolf Serkin, The New York Philharmonic Orchestra/
   Leonard Bernstein
Sony Classical SK 63080

LUDWIG VAN BEETHOVEN (1770–1827):
Piano Sonatas – "Moonlight," "Waldstein," "Appassionata"

When Beethoven moved to Vienna, audiences there had never heard a pianist quite like him before. Pianists of the day were usually steeped in eighteenth-century style and tradition, which valued clarity, restraint, and elegance. Beethoven was probably never a great virtuoso, but he brought a power and energy to piano playing unheard of by the Viennese until then. His style was forceful, confident, and on a larger scale, with a driving momentum. Beethoven was also an improviser like no other. Improvisation was one of the stocks in trade of a late eighteenth-century pianist, and expected by audiences. Most pianists could extemporize on a popular tune and had reams of impressive passagework prepared that they could knock off at will. But Beethoven brought a more personal and original tone to his improvisations. Once he got going, the ideas flowed one after the other, often becoming quite emotional and passionate. Beethoven was a more active and freer pianist at the keyboard, his hands and arms coming down from on high. The delicate keyboard instruments of the day had been designed for gentle use, hands held just above the keyboard with the fingers doing most of the work. But Beethoven demanded more from a piano, and strings often snapped and hammers became stuck or broke under the force of his playing.

The sonatas on this recommended recording are three of the most popular and clearly show the innovation and originality that Beethoven brought to piano music. The "Moonlight" Sonata is so-named because a music critic likened the calm of the first movement to moonlight on Lake Lucerne. The galloping, frenzied third movement must have been some of the wildest music ever heard at the time.

The Piano Sonata, Op. 53 by Beethoven carries the nickname "Waldstein" because of the dedicatee. Count Ferdinand Waldstein was a friend and patron of Beethoven from his years in Bonn. The sonata dates from the early years of the nineteenth century, the period when Beethoven had come to grips with his increasing deafness. Realizing that one day he would be stone deaf, the "Waldstein" sonata focused the frustration of his illness and forced him to become all the more determined to overcome it. This sonata and the "Appassionata" were the first to take advantage of the extended keyboard on a piano given to Beethoven by the Paris piano manufacturer Erard in 1803.

Parallels have often been made between the Symphony No. 5 by Beethoven and the Piano Sonata, Op. 57, "Appassionata." They are both in a minor key, both have a surging, passionate power, and both make considerable demands on the performers.

Mikhail Pletnev is the kind of pianist who forces you to listen to him – not unlike Beethoven in his early days in Vienna. Pletnev has never been satisfied with the tried and true, and his interpretations of these three popular Beethoven sonatas show confidence and power in the fast movements, and depth of emotion in the slow movements. They are excellent examples of Beethoven's middle period.

■ ───────────────────────

LUDWIG VAN BEETHOVEN: *Piano Sonatas – "Moonlight,"*
   "Waldstein," "Appassionata"
Mikhail Pletnev
Virgin Classics   561 834-2

LUDWIG VAN BEETHOVEN (1770–1827):
String Quartets Op. 59, Nos. 1–3, Op. 74, "Harp"

In his music, Beethoven stretched the musical practices and styles that he inherited from his predecessors Haydn and Mozart. By giving his music a new force and momentum on a grander scale, with more emotional power, Beethoven stretched the traits of the Classical period to their limits, opening the door to the nineteenth-century Romantic Age. By the late eighteenth century, the string quartet had evolved into an established, cultured field – the pre-eminent chamber music form. But it was all to be changed by Beethoven.

His life is usually grouped into three main creative periods – early, middle, and late. In the string quartets of the early period (to about 1800), he continued the eighteenth-century style, but increased its expressive and emotional elements, pushing them to their boundaries. In the middle period quartets, starting around 1804, he moved even further away from the Classical period models, increasing the length, momentum, originality, and intensity of the music. And in the late period quartets, the content and expression of the music tended to dictate the form, and there is a spirituality present that was new to chamber music.

The three string quartets of Op. 59 were commissioned in 1805 by Count Andreas Razumovsky, the Russian Ambassador to the Hapsburg Court in Vienna and one of the city's most important musical patrons. They have become universally known as the Razumovsky Quartets. The reception they received in Vienna was one of the poorest Beethoven received for any of his works. People laughed during the performance, believing that Beethoven was playing jokes on them. When a violinist said to Beethoven, "Surely you do not consider this music," the composer was reported to have said cruelly, "No, not for you, but for a later age." Nothing could have been closer to the truth. As in other music from Beethoven's middle period, such as the Symphony No. 3 "Eroica," the opera *Fidelio*, and the "Appassionata" Piano Sonata, the Razumovsky Quartets show a new confidence and assurance and signpost the direction of Beethoven's later compositions.

The String Quartet in E-flat, Op. 74, has the nickname "Harp," because of the pizzicato or plucked string passages in the first movement. In this work, almost as if he were consciously backing off from some of the innovations in the Razumovsky Quartets, Beethoven is more constrained. All the same, and typical of Beethoven, he is unhappy resting on his laurels. The opening passages of Op. 74 are quiet and devotional, but they are followed by surprises. The finale is a set of variations – the only time Beethoven used the variation form to close one of his quartets.

The Takacs Quartet, originally from Budapest, began to record the complete String Quartets by Beethoven for Decca in 2002, and its first release was the middle period quartets. Its clear, clean lines, warm passion, and unwavering control and balance clearly show a quartet at the pinnacle of its powers.

■ ─────────────────────────────────────

LUDWIG VAN BEETHOVEN: *String Quartets, Op. 59,*
  Nos. 1–3, Op. 74, "Harp"
Takacs Quartet
Decca 470 847-2

LUDWIG VAN BEETHOVEN (1770–1827): Symphony No. 9 in D Minor, Op. 125, "Choral"

Few composers felt and reflected the social changes happening around them better than Beethoven. He lived at a time of great change, as the ancient feudal system in Europe began to break down, and the rise of the middle class began to take hold. The French Revolution and the ideals of liberty, equality, and brotherhood were close to his heart, and they encouraged him to develop new styles of expression. As a result, his late works show a greater freedom in all aspects of music-making, from overall design to internal form and structure, emotion and expression.

The Symphony No. 9 by Beethoven is the classic example. It's a work that presents a struggle against oppression that's ultimately victorious, similar to his Symphony No. 5. But in the Ninth, the subject is humanity in general. It expresses Beethoven's vision of a perfect society, instilled with friendship, happiness, and a loving God in heaven. These are the reasons why the Beethoven Ninth has often been performed at historical occasions calling for heroism and optimism, like the fall of the Berlin Wall in 1989.

To achieve these lofty goals, Beethoven added to the orchestra four vocal soloists and a choir in the finale, something that had never been done before. Many of his contemporaries felt he was mad to break down traditional forms and end the separation between the genres of choral music and symphonic music. Others thought that he had cheapened symphonic music, and that the choral finale was a huge miscalculation. But Beethoven needed these innovations to realize the higher level to which he wanted to take music. Every composer of symphonies that followed couldn't help but be influenced.

The choral finale has become so popular today, listeners often overlook the previous three movements, as well as the beginning of the finale before the vocal elements enter. But everything in the Ninth has its place and prepares us for the finale.

The huge first movement sets the stage for the struggle. Richard Wagner described it as "the soul contending for happiness against the oppression of that inimical power that places itself between us and the joys of the earth." The second movement has dance qualities, but it's a violent, driven dance, so wild with energy that we worry it might get off-track. The third, slow movement seems to suspend time and space, and creates a spiritual quality that has rarely been matched. Then we arrive at the finale. From his sketches of the work, it's clear that Beethoven wrestled with how to incorporate the soloists and choir. He finally came up with the perfect solution by using a series of flashbacks. After the raucous opening, representing turmoil and anarchy, the cellos and double basses enter in recitative style, a vocal style based on the natural rhythmic inflections of speech. They lead the orchestra in retracing music from the previous movements, in search of potential material. But it's all refused. Finally, snippets of the famous "Ode to Joy" theme are brought forward, agreed upon, and developed. Beethoven then brings back the cacophony of the opening of the movement, before the bass soloist enters with a call to unite. What follows is well known – Beethoven's setting of the "Ode to Joy" by Friedrich Schiller, which ends the symphony as a triumphant and euphoric hymn of praise, uniting all mankind.

George Szell led the Cleveland Orchestra for almost a quarter century and turned it into one of the finest in the world. He used to boast that the orchestra began to rehearse where others left off. The result was a highly disciplined ensemble that combined a rich orchestral sonority with the clarity and balance of chamber music. This 1961 recording caught them at the peak, in a performance of fire and gripping magnetism. Everyone involved, from orchestral members to soloists to the choir, sat up in their chairs and gave Szell their all. Beethoven's message has rarely been more clearly or more thrillingly presented.

∎ _____

LUDWIG VAN BEETHOVEN: *Symphony No. 9 in D Minor,*
   Op. 125, "Choral"
Cleveland Orchestra/George Szell
Sony Classical   SK 89959

LUDWIG VAN BEETHOVEN (1770–1827):
Violin Concerto in D, Op. 61

This concerto by Beethoven was the first of the so-called great nineteenth-century violin concertos. Later works include those by Mendelssohn, Brahms, Tchaikovsky, and others. The big difference between what came before and the Beethoven concerto is the treatment of the solo violin and the orchestra. Eighteenth-century violin concertos often relied heavily on the repeated alternation of soloist and orchestra. But in Beethoven's Violin Concerto, we are presented with a work where the soloist and the orchestra are more closely integrated into the overall orchestral fabric. Also, the Beethoven concerto mostly eschews virtuosic display for the soloist and concentrates more on a solid musical fable that has a solo violin and an orchestra as protagonists.

Maybe it was this lack of display in the work that prompted the violinist at the first performance in Vienna in 1806 to take matters into his own hands. Typical of Beethoven, the score was not ready in time for rehearsal. So the talented young Viennese violinist Franz Clement had to play the piece from sight at the premiere, which apparently he did quite well. But between the first and second movements of the concerto, Clement performed a short piece of his own, on one string while holding the violin upside down! Perhaps Beethoven even expected this kind of stunt from Clement, because on the manuscript score, he pleaded for clemency by writing a clever pun: "Concerto par Clemenza pour Clement."

From most reports, the concerto was warmly received by the public in 1806, but it subsequently suffered under harsh criticism for decades. Some critics found that, although it did contain some beauty, the continuity of the work was often broken by repetitions of ho-hum material. Others picked up on Beethoven's use of kettledrums in the work and jokingly referred to it as "Concerto for Kettledrum." But eventually it was taken up by the great nineteenth-century violin virtuoso Joseph Joachim, for whom Brahms was to later write his violin concerto. In Joachim's hands, at the midpoint of the century, the Beethoven concerto gained its proper respect and status. Today, it is one of the most popular of all works for violin and orchestra, and recognized as the first "great" violin concerto of symphonic scope and grandeur.

Itzhak Perlman has recorded the Violin Concerto in D a couple of times – this is the first, done in 1980, in the early days of digital recording. He and conductor Carlo Maria Giulini are of like minds here, offering a concerto that is proud, noble, and majestic, warm and deeply felt. Perlman's tone is typically large, and he plays with a freedom and ease that maintain interest throughout. The slow movement gives off a relaxed, contented beauty, while the finale is a high-spirited but controlled dance. The rich recorded sound only enhances the performance.

■ ───

LUDWIG VAN BEETHOVEN: *Violin Concerto in D, Op. 61*
Itzhak Perlman, Philharmonia Orchestra/Carlo Maria Giulini
EMI Classics 566 900-2

GIOACHINO ROSSINI (1792–1868):
Overtures, Highlights from Il Barbiere di Siviglia

If the purpose of an opera overture is to prepare the audience for the mood and emotions of the opera that follows, Rossini was a master. By the time any Rossini overture ends and the curtain rises, our anticipation for the opera has increased, and we are on our way to an evening of enjoyment. Part of the reason for its success is the musical invention now known as the "Rossini crescendo." This is a long, carefully paced progression from soft to loud. Simple maybe, but its effect is the enhancement of the dramatic tension. It's an infectious trick, but one that works well, and Rossini used it often.

And yet, to Rossini, the overture to an opera was almost an afterthought. He usually composed them last – often just before the premiere. He once quipped, "Nothing primes inspiration more than necessity." For his 1817 opera *La gazza ladra* (*The Thieving Magpie*), he composed the overture on the day of the opening. The stage director literally imprisoned Rossini in the theatre. As Rossini composed the overture, he was guarded by stagehands who dropped the score, page by page, out the window to the copyists below, who then rushed to the orchestra for rehearsal. It's said that the stage director was so angry with Rossini, he instructed the stagehands to throw him out the window if the pages of the overture ever stopped coming!

Together with Gaetano Donizetti (1797–1848) and Vincenzo Bellini (1801–1835), Rossini is considered one of the great composers of *bel canto* – beautiful singing. This was an Italian vocal style of the eighteenth and nineteenth centuries that focused on elegance, beautiful tone, shapely phrasing, and florid and effortless delivery. In *bel canto*, the beauty of the vocal sound and the brilliance of the singer outweigh the dramatic expression and emotion.

Rossini had a gift for turning out music that perfectly suited the voice and drama of opera, as well as catching the human element – from deep love, to grief and loss, to slapstick humour. He dominated the opera world in Europe in the first few decades of the nineteenth century. Then, in his late thirties, at the height of his powers and fame, he gave it all up. After a string of almost forty operatic successes in less than twenty years, Rossini wrote nothing more for the stage. In the last thirty-nine years of his life, he composed only a few sacred works, some songs, and a handful of light piano pieces. He died a wealthy man in 1868.

As was most of his music, Rossini was known for his humour and wit, and anecdotes and stories about him abound. Once, a young composer approached him for advice and presented two new compositions. After Rossini had heard the first, he quickly turned to the boy and said, "I like the other one better."

The recommended recording features seven of Rossini's opera overtures, as well as three vocal excerpts from probably his most popular opera: *The Barber of Seville*. Conductor Gianluigi Gelmetti is a Roman who has made a name for himself across Europe for his performances of Rossini. He brings sparkle and vivacity to the music, but with good control, nice pacing, and the necessary wit.

■ ──────────────────────────────────

GIOACHINO ROSSINI: *Overtures, Highlights from Il Barbiere di Siviglia*
Radio Symphony Orchestra of Stuttgart/Gianluigi Gelmetti
EMI Classics Encores   574 752-2

FRANZ SCHUBERT (1797–1828):
Lieder

With the burgeoning of the Romantic movement in the early years of the nineteenth century came a greater awareness of personal emotions and expression. One of the results was a new form of lyric poetry that spotlighted the individual's objective perspective and the poetic concept. The form of the poem was now less important than its emotional content, and became subservient to it. From the poetry evolved the *lied*, or German art song.

Franz Schubert was one of the greatest of all classical song composers and is often credited with inventing the lied. It's not quite true, for earlier composers, even Schubert's idol, Beethoven, had composed secular songs. But Schubert wrote so many of them and developed the characteristics and qualities of the lied so much that it was never the same after him. No longer was the song merely words set to a melody and presented by a singer with piano accompaniment. It was a new, powerful form of song that treated text, singer, and pianist equally. It was not so much *how* Schubert set poetry to music – but how he translated the poetry *into* music.

A good example is the early song "Der Erlkönig" or "The Erlking," based on a poem by Goethe and composed by Schubert while he was still a teenager. The piano paints the picture of a galloping horse in a raging storm, adding tension and anxiety. The singer must play the roles of four different characters: a narrator, the child, the calming father, and the evil Erlking. Text, singer, and pianist all come together to express the terror of the child, the father's concern and soothing reassurance, and the dastardly leer of the Erlking. At the end, the galloping figures in the piano slow, as the child lies dead in his father's arms. It's almost like a four-minute operatic scene.

In his short life of only thirty-one years, Schubert composed well over six hundred songs. Even more impressive is their consistently high quality – from his first fresh, youthful songs written as a teenager to the mature, masterful songs of his final year. Schubert was also the first to realize the power of song cycles, a collection of individually complete songs linked together by a narrative thread or common theme. The advances that Schubert made to the form of song helped other composers recognize the power of the lied, and its tradition and legacy have continued to the present day.

One of the greatest lieder singers of the twentieth century was the German baritone Dietrich Fischer-Dieskau, and one of the great song pianists (the role is too important for the term accompanist) was Gerald Moore. Fischer-Dieskau had a gorgeous baritone voice, a quick mind, solid musicianship, and the ability to communicate. Moore was with him every step of the way. They later recorded the complete Schubert songs together, but this collection of twenty-one is a gem. Recorded in the late 1950s and 1960s, when Fischer-Dieskau was in his prime, these two musicians set a standard that will be difficult to match.

■

FRANZ SCHUBERT: *Lieder*
Dietrich Fischer-Dieskau, Gerald Moore
EMI Classics Encore   574 754-2

Franz Schubert (1797–1828):
Piano Quintet in A, D. 667, "Trout"

In the summer of 1819, Schubert spent part of his vacation on a walking tour of Upper Austria with his friend, the singer Michael Vogl. It was one of the happiest times of Schubert's life. They were based in the small town of Steyr, Vogl's hometown, not far from Linz, and boarded at a home with hosts who had several attractive daughters. Schubert wrote to his brother, "At the house where I lodge there are eight girls, nearly all pretty. Plenty to do, you see."

Summer evenings in Steyr were often spent with wine, music, and song at the home of Sylvester Paumgartner, a mining engineer who was a good amateur cellist and chamber music fan. At one point, Paumgartner asked Schubert to compose a chamber work that would include a set of variations on Schubert's song from two years earlier, *Die Forelle* or "The Trout." There was one other condition. Paumgartner also requested that the work be scored for the same instruments as the Piano Quintet, Op. 87, by Johann Nepomuk Hummel, a work that was a favourite of Paumgartner's and his chamber music collaborators. The Hummel piano quintet was unusually scored for piano, violin, viola, cello, and double bass. The more standard instrumentation of a piano quintet is piano with string quartet, or two violins, viola, and cello. Schubert had no objections to the stipulations, set to the task immediately, and the new work was completed back in Vienna that fall.

The result is one of the best-loved chamber music works of all time – the "Trout" Quintet, a piece brimming over with youthful zest, happiness, and warm summer mountain breezes. It contains a total of five movements instead of the usual four – two outer fast movements, and two inner slow movements that frame a middle movement scherzo. The second of the slow movements is the one that features the variations on the Schubert song, "The Trout," stipulated by Paumgartner. Schubert puts the song through six variations, after stating the theme at the outset. In the first three variations, he passes the tune, in order, to the piano, viola and cello, and then to the double bass, with elaborations and ornamentations from the others. The fourth and fifth variations are more involved, with the original tune a little more obscured. And in the sixth and final variation, Schubert, saving the best for last, alternates the tune between the violin and cello, while the piano has the rippling accompaniment so familiar from the original Schubert song.

Although the recording quality of the 1958 recording with pianist Sir Clifford Curzon and members of the Vienna Octet leaves a little to be desired, this is a classic performance of the "Trout" Quintet. Schubert's Viennese style is evident all through it, due in part to the inclusion of the Vienna Philharmonic's concertmaster at the time, Willi Boskovsky. The piano can often drown out the others in this instrumental makeup, but Curzon's keen chamber music ear never allows that to happen. There's an awareness, love, and joy in the delicate clarity and refinement of one of Schubert's masterpieces.

■ ——————————————————————————————————

FRANZ SCHUBERT: *Piano Quintet in A, D. 667, "Trout"*
Sir Clifford Curzon, members of the Vienna Octet
Decca Eloquence   467 417-2

FRANZ SCHUBERT (1797–1828):
Symphonies Nos. 8 & 9

The reason why Schubert left his Symphony No. 8 "unfinished" with only two movements, is one of the great mysteries of music. Death wasn't the cause, because Schubert was to live for another six years, and even composed another symphony, which he did complete. One speculation has it that the two existing movements showed too many similarities to the Symphony No. 2 by Beethoven, and Schubert was worried he would be accused of copying his idol. Another says that he did complete the symphony, but the last two movements were lost. Still another theory has Schubert composing the symphony for someone he had fallen in love with, and when spurned, he dropped it. But maybe the most soothing theory is that, after writing the two powerful existing movements, Schubert couldn't match them and lost interest in the work. The incomplete score lay dormant for decades. The premiere of the "Unfinished" was finally heard in Vienna in 1865, thirty-three years after Schubert's death.

In the nineteenth century, some conductors borrowed movements from other Schubert symphonies to wrap it up. But today, performances feature just the two movements Schubert left us. Music lovers embraced the work anyway, despite its incompleteness. Maybe it's a little like the Venus de Milo. If we now found the arms to add to the famous torso, would we appreciate the piece any better?

The Symphony No. 9 in C by Schubert has the nickname "Great" to distinguish it from the earlier symphony No. 6 in the same key, known as the "Little." Although the No. 9 was completed by the composer, it suffered from the other unfortunate fate – being performed. It was rehearsed to be performed in Vienna, most likely before Schubert's death in 1828, but the orchestra rejected it, declaring it too long and difficult. Later, after Schubert had died, orchestras in Paris and London rejected it for the same reasons. The finale on its own was heard in Vienna in 1836. Then in 1838, Robert Schumann managed to obtain the score from Schubert's brother, and had it sent to Felix Mendelssohn in Leipzig. It was first performed complete in Leipzig in 1839, conducted by Mendelssohn. In his review of the premiere, Schumann made the now-famous comment about the symphony's "heavenly length," probably to challenge the belief that the work was too long. But the romantic Schumann also went on to say, "More than merely lovely melody, something above and beyond sorrow and joy lies concealed in this symphony. . . . We are transported by the music to a region where we can never remember to have been before."

Karl Böhm conducted the symphonies by Schubert often during his career, and was known for his clean lines and a light touch. These recordings of Nos. 8 and 9 were made in the 1960s, and the Berlin Philharmonic gave Böhm performances that have become legendary. They are warm and dramatic, with that all-important sense of musical line that differentiates mediocre Schubert performances from great ones. At a budget price, these recordings are incomparable.

■ ──

FRANZ SCHUBERT: *Symphonies Nos. 8 & 9*
Berlin Philharmonic Orchestra/Karl Böhm
DGG Eloquence   469 627-2

FRANZ SCHUBERT (1797–1828):
Piano Sonata in B-flat, D. 960, etc.

It's often been said that Schubert's great gift was for melody. All of his music, in large or small forms, is instilled with a wealth of lyrical tunes of incomparable beauty. Schubert claimed that he was only just able to get one melody down on paper before another one entered his mind. Many of his songs and shorter piano pieces were composed in a single flash of creativity.

It's melody that is the predominant trait of the final piano sonata Schubert wrote in 1828, within months of his death. Although he composed some twenty piano sonatas, many were left incomplete, as Schubert seemed to struggle with the larger sonata structure. But melody wins out in this last sonata, and arguments about structure and form, the development of ideas, can easily be brushed aside.

Although the Sonata in B-flat is on a big scale, some thirty-five or forty minutes in length, at its essence it is intimate and personal. The first three movements all begin and end quietly. The first movement has an eerie calm to its gorgeous opening theme, which ends mysteriously with an ominous trill in the bass. It's as if Schubert is saying that all is not as it may seem. The slow second movement is the emotional heart of the sonata. The gentle lilting accompaniment only enhances the haunting, nostalgic qualities. The middle section is more confident and assured, but the dark song returns to close in quiet despair. The scherzo breaks the mood brightly, but the middle section here is the one with the dark overtones. On the surface, the last movement seems jocular with its opening exposed first note returning often to break up the momentum. But there's more to come, as Schubert creates tension in the play between major and minor, as well as between the lyrical and the vigorous.

It was Schubert who developed the term *Moments musicaux*, musical moments. They are short, simple pieces that give the impression of being improvised on the spur of the moment. The third of the set, sometimes called "Air Russe," is one of Schubert's most popular compositions, and it has frequently been transcribed for other instruments. The *Moments musicaux* were very popular in nineteenth-century homes, when amateur music-making was at its peak, before the arrival of movies, radio, and television.

Wilhelm Kempff was "old school" and proud of his links to the past. His teacher had studied with von Bülow, who had studied with Liszt, who had studied with Czerny, who had studied with Beethoven. As a student, Kempff majored in philosophy as well as music, and he was a composer himself. Everything he did seemed to have a context. Kempff recorded the complete Schubert sonatas in the 1960s, and this recording of the final sonata is the crown of the set. There's a simple unadorned beauty to his Schubert, that stresses warm expression and avoids sentimentality.

■ ──

FRANZ SCHUBERT: *Piano Sonata in B-flat, D. 960, etc.*
Wilhelm Kempff
DGG Eloquence　469 668-2

HECTOR BERLIOZ (1803–1869):
Symphonie fantastique

The French composer Hector Berlioz was the epitome of the early Romantic period: temperamental, even flighty, spontaneous, passionate, intense, and highly imaginative. And Berlioz lived at a time when music, and the public's perception of music, were witnessing huge changes. The American and French Revolutions, initiated the demise of nobles and the aristocracy, and the rise of human rights and the middle class. Not long afterward, the Industrial Revolution brought about a shift from rural to urban life, and with it the performance of music moved from the palaces and salons of the aristocracy to public concert halls. Composers became less interested in fulfilling the wishes of patrons. In Beethoven's hands, encouraged by the romantic ideals of the burgeoning nineteenth century, musical composition had evolved into a vehicle of self-expression, rather than mere entertainment.

Although Berlioz was unable to play any instrument very well, he became one of the great symphonists of all time, and it's due to one single work – the *Symphonie fantastique*, a work of incredible imagination, originality, and power. In 1827, Berlioz took in a staging of Shakespeare's *Hamlet* in Paris. The Irish actress Harriet Smithson played the role of Ophelia. To say that Berlioz fell in love with Smithson would be an understatement – obsession would be more accurate. He called on her, wrote her letters, and hounded her. Understandably, she rejected his advances. In 1830, in frustration, Berlioz composed the *Symphonie fantastique*, a musical depiction (and self-portrait) of a young man in love. In a detailed program that accompanies the symphony, Berlioz laid out the story of infatuation at a lavish ball, a lonely scene in the country, an hallucinogenic dream where the hero kills his beloved and then witnesses his own execution, and a witches' orgy where the beloved appears as a grotesque vision. Harriet Smithson eventually agreed to meet Berlioz, and in 1833 they were married. However, the marriage failed, and the two separated in 1840.

In the *Symphonie fantastique*, the beloved is represented by an *idée fixe*, a fixed idea. This is a compositional technique where a specific tune or motif is attached to a person or idea. Then, by altering and transforming the *idée fixe*, the composer can suggest changes in the character of the person, or changes in the perception of that person. For example, when the *idée fixe* appears in the first movement, it's demure and timid. But when it shows up in the fifth and final movement during the witches' Sabbath, the noble, demure traits are gone, and it appears as grotesque, mocking, and distorted. Berlioz combined infatuation, frustration, skill, and a vivid imagination to produce one of the most original works in the repertoire, a true showpiece for orchestra.

Sir Colin Davis has always been a great champion and advocate of the music of Berlioz, and his 1974 recording of the *Symphonie fantastique* with the Concertgebouw Orchestra is one of the finest ever made. Both the performance and the recording are vividly alive and colourful. Davis is able to combine the passionate with control. Although each episode in the life of the artist is clearly individual, there is always a sense of purpose and overall structure to the entire work.

■

HECTOR BERLIOZ: *Symphonie fantastique*
Royal Concertgebouw Orchestra of Amsterdam/Sir Colin Davis
Philips   464 692-2

FELIX MENDELSSOHN (1809–1847):
Octet in E-flat, Op. 20

Like Mozart and Schubert before him, Felix Mendelssohn was a child prodigy. By the age of ten he could play several instruments well, compose, speak and read several languages, write poetry, and even paint. While he was growing up, the Mendelssohn family home in Berlin was a hub for the best of Berlin's musicians, as well as others who stopped in the city on concert tours. On Sunday mornings, there were often gatherings and informal musical per formances. It's believed that Mendelssohn composed his Octet for Strings for one such Sunday get-together in 1825, when he was sixteen years old. He probably played one of the viola parts in the first performance. The Octet is one of the finest compositions in all music written by one so young – even more mature than the music that Mozart or Schubert had written by the same age. Later, Mendelssohn referred to the work as one of his personal favourites, saying, "I had a most wonderful time writing it!"

The Mendelssohn Octet is scored for double string quartet, or four violins, two violas, and two cellos. But despite this chamber music scoring, on each of the parts Mendelssohn instructed the player to perform in the style of a symphony. It's obvious that he wanted the delicacy of a chamber music piece, with the depth and variety of colours of a symphony.

The third movement scherzo is the best-known movement, sometimes played on its own as a showpiece by orchestral string sections. In style and mood, it's a forerunner of the famous Overture to *A Midsummer Night's Dream* by Mendelssohn, composed a year later. According to Mendelssohn's sister Fanny, the inspiration for the scherzo came from a scene from Goethe's *Faust* that ends:

> Flight of clouds and trail of mist,
> Are lighted from above,
> A breeze in the leaves, a wind in the reeds,
> And all is blown away.

Fanny wrote of the movement, "The whole piece is to be played staccato and pianissimo with shivering tremolos and lightning flashes of trills. All is new, strange and yet so familiar and pleasing – one feels so close to the world of spirits, lightly carried away up into the air. Indeed one might take a broomstick so as to follow the airy procession. At the end, the first violin soars feather-light aloft, and all is blown away." It's no wonder that this movement led to some of the adjectives often used to describe Mendelssohn's delicate style: gossamer, wispy, elfin, feathery, and effervescent. In the finale, the scherzo returns briefly, before the movement rushes to its jubilant end.

The Academy of St-Martin-in-the-Fields Chamber Ensemble is a group of talented musicians who are used to playing together. This recording is the most successful in achieving Mendelssohn's wish of combining chamber music with the sound of a symphony. The playing is fresh, tight, and articulate with sparkling ensemble work, all within a symphonic style. The warm recorded sound nicely catches the rich string sound of the ensemble.

■──

FELIX MENDELSSOHN: *Octet in E-flat, Op. 20*
Academy of St. Martin-in-the-Fields Chamber Ensemble
Philips   420 400-2

FELIX MENDELSSOHN (1809–1847): *Symphonies Nos. 3 & 4*

The names "Scottish" and "Italian" attached to Symphonies Nos. 3 and 4 by Mendelssohn, respectively, have more to do with the inspirational locations, than the use of Scottish or Italian tunes and idioms. The opening of the Symphony No. 3 may conjure up mists and rain, evoking heroic Scottish legends, and it was the warm, sunny qualities of the Symphony No. 4, more than anything else, that led to its title of "Italian." Mendelssohn was always reluctant to explain his music or suggest programs, and no less a musician than composer Robert Schumann has been confused. After hearing a performance of the "Scottish" Symphony, which he believed was the "Italian," Schumann waxed on about the Italian landscape he heard drawn in the music and remarked, "It is so beautiful as to compensate a listener who had never been to Italy." As always, we should listen to the music for what it is, and not be too concerned with extra-musical titles or notions.

The Symphony No. 3 was conceived during Mendelssohn's visit to Scotland in 1829. He was impressed with the barren landscape, the rugged coastline, and the rich heritage of Scottish history and culture. After visiting Holyrood in Edinburgh, the ruined palace of Mary Queen of Scots, he wrote, "In the evening twilight, we went today to the palace where Queen Mary lived and loved. The chapel is now roofless, grass and ivy grow there, and at that broken altar Mary was crowned Queen of Scotland. Everything around is broken and mouldering, and the bright sky shines in. I believe I found today the source of my Scottish symphony." Mendelssohn's *Hebrides* Overture or "Fingal's Cave" was also inspired by this Scottish journey.

A little over a year after returning from Scotland, Mendelssohn travelled to Italy to soak up Italian culture. This time he wrote, "The whole country has such a festive air that I felt as if I were a young prince making his entry." While in Rome, Mendelssohn made sketches for a new symphony that in general terms would catch the spirit of Italy and the temperament of the people. It was only once he was back in Germany that he really buckled down to the work, composing the Symphony No. 4, side by side with the No. 3, finishing the Fourth first. He conducted the premiere in London in 1833, but despite its immediate success, Mendelssohn was dissatisfied, and it was withheld from publication until after his death.

Claudio Abbado brings much life and energy to the Mendelssohn symphonies, and these recordings are some of his finest, made during the 1980s when he was music director of the London Symphony Orchestra. The strings bite into their parts happily, and there's clear, bright work from the winds and brass. The vitality created gives one a sense of the dust being brushed off these well-loved warhorses.

■ ────────────────────────────────

FELIX MENDELSSOHN: *Symphonies Nos. 3 & 4*
London Symphony Orchestra/Claudio Abbado
DGG   427 810-2

ROBERT SCHUMANN (1810–1856):
Dichterliebe, Op. 48

Robert Schumann was one of the most romantic of the early Romantic composers. Where others drew their inspiration from external sources, from nature, history, or folk legends, Schumann found his passionate fire in his own personality and experiences.

As a young man, Schumann showed the potential for a brilliant career as a concert pianist and began to study with the noted Leipzig piano teacher Friedrich Wieck. Schumann spent long hours practising, and even created a device that was supposed to strengthen the fourth finger of his right hand. But the contraption backfired and permanently damaged Schumann's finger, forcing him to give up on the idea of a performing career and concentrate on composing. At the same time, his eye began to fall on Wieck's young daughter, Clara. Before long the two were madly in love, much against Wieck's wishes. It was one thing for Wieck to treat Schumann, his most talented student, as a son – it was another thing to consider him a future son-in-law. After Wieck had unsuccessfully tried just about everything to break up the two lovers, even the courts, Clara and Robert were finally married in 1840.

The result of the new-found bliss was a huge outpouring of songs or *lieder* from Schumann. Almost half of all the songs he composed in his lifetime were penned in the year 1840. The vocal field was one in which Schumann was very comfortable and easily inspired. As a young man, he had written poetry and set it to his own music. A good writer and critic on musical topics, Schumann became the influential editor of a prominent music journal. With his knowledge of poetry, writing, and music, he had a great sympathy and gift for setting words to music. He wrote, "I can hardly tell you what a pleasure it is to write for the voice compared with instrumental composition, and how this rages and wells up within me."

One of the major works to emerge out of Schumann's 1840 "song" year was the cycle *Dichterliebe*, or "The Poet's Love," to poetry by Heinrich Heine. The sixteen songs in the cycle follow a narrative line of the poet's awakening to the joys of love, through rejection, and eventual heartbreak. Schumann was the heir to the legacy of Franz Schubert, taking the form of the song cycle even further. The overall expression and emotional content were broadened and often became more intense. The role of the piano was increased, with preludes or postludes for the piano alone, often with musical material not included in the song, created to capture mood or to comment or suggest further insights into the essence of the poem.

German baritone Matthias Goerne studied with soprano Elisabeth Schwarzkopf and baritone Dietrich Fischer-Dieskau, and continues the great German tradition of *Lieder* singing. Like his teachers, Goerne combines beauty of tone with intelligence and insight, and *Dichterliebe*'s yearning, sorrow, and regret are brought across beautifully. Rarely has the brooding and bitter character of the cycle been as strongly conveyed. Pianist Vladimir Ashkenazy, a strong Schumann pianist and no stranger to lieder, is an experienced and supportive partner.

ROBERT SCHUMANN: *Dichterliebe, Op. 48*
Matthias Goerne, Vladimir Ashkenazy
Decca   289 458 2652

ROBERT SCHUMANN (1810–1856):
Kinderszenen, Kreisleriana, Humoreske

In the year 1840, newly married and very much in love, Robert Schumann dove almost exclusively into the composition of songs. In the previous ten years, Schumann had focused almost entirely on music for solo piano, his own instrument, and after 1840, he concentrated on orchestral music, then chamber music, then choral music and opera. Three of his greatest works for piano date from the years 1838–1839: *Kinderszenen*, *Kreisleriana*, and the *Humoreske*, Op. 20.

Kinderszenen or *Scenes from Childhood* is another of Schumann's works composed under the inspiration of his wife, Clara. Throughout his life, Schumann maintained a childlike innocence and sense of wonder, which often led to misunderstanding and criticism. These childlike traits are part of the attraction of Schumann, but also the pitfalls. He wrote to Clara during the composition:

> Perhaps it was an echo of what you once said to me, that sometimes I seemed to you like a child. These scenes are peaceful, tender and happy, like our future. You will enjoy them, but of course, you will have to forget that you are a virtuoso.

Kinderszenen was not meant for children. They are more like "reminiscences of a grown-up for grown-ups," as Schumann himself put it. They are quite different in tone and sophistication from his later *Album for the Young*, Op. 68, composed for his own children to play. The No. 7, *Träumerei* or *Reverie* is one of the all-time "hits" for the piano.

Kreisleriana was composed about six weeks after *Kinderszenen* in 1838, over a period of about four days. Once again, Clara was his inspiration, and Schumann told her that she was the subject of the work. The title comes from the character of Johannes Kreisler, an eccentric, wild but clever musician created by E.T.A. Hoffmann, with whom Schumann identified. Like *Kinderszenen*, *Kreisleriana* too contains childlike innocence, but here there's also a darker, deeper side, with Schumann pouring out more of his own inner emotions. As he wrote to Clara, "Play my *Kreisleriana* once in a while. You will find a wild, unbridled love, together with your life and mine."

The *Humoreske* dates from 1839 and was also written in a fit of inspiration, this time, in about a week. Like *Kreisleriana*, Schumann's quick-changing extremes of moods are evident once more, although the episodes here follow one another without break, in one continuous movement. The title "Humoreske" has always caused some confusion and Schumann himself compounded the problem by claiming that the piece was "not very cheerful, perhaps my most melancholy work." Although there are witty elements in it, there are also many other moods and emotions, often breaking in abruptly. To Schumann, inner emotions could be successfully explored through the distance of irony and humour. The *Humoreske* has always tended to be more of a favourite with pianists than audiences, but the work has gained popularity in recent decades and is increasingly recognized as one of Schumann's greatest creations.

The challenge in playing Schumann's piano music is to bring across the quixotic emotions without sounding flighty and insincere. Radu Lupu is one of the great Schumann pianists, creating beautiful individual miniatures but within an overall unified scheme and structure. His masterful blend of virtuosity and poetry combines to present a natural and unforced authority in this often elusive repertoire.

■

ROBERT SCHUMANN: *Kinderszenen, Kreisleriana, Humoreske*
Radu Lupu
Decca 440 496-2

FRÉDÉRIC CHOPIN (1810–1849):
Piano Concerto No. 1 in E Minor, Op. 11, etc.

The name of Chopin is indelibly and inextricably linked with the piano. Nearly all the music he composed features the piano, and the remainder of it includes the piano. No other composer has devoted himself to that instrument as much as he, and few others have contributed as much to its literature. Where Beethoven was often orchestral in his approach to the piano, and Schubert vocal, Chopin was always pianistic. There are few piano recitals today that don't include a work by him, and quite a few are all-Chopin. Although many of his great melodies for the piano have been transcribed for a variety of other instruments, something is always lost in the translation. It's the idiom of the piano that was always front and centre in Chopin's compositions. After Robert Schumann heard Chopin play, he announced, "Hats off, gentlemen. A genius!"

Chopin composed both of his piano concertos in Poland, before leaving his native land to settle permanently in Paris. The Piano Concerto No. 1 in E Minor was actually the second composed but the first published, hence the reason for the numbering. Both concertos were criticized at the time for the limited role of the orchestra. Many nineteenth-century concertos created interest and drama through a conflict between soloist and orchestra: the individual against the masses. But Chopin was quite content to have the piano shine throughout, leaving the orchestra to play a subservient, accompanying role, or as the introducer of musical material before the piano makes its entry. It's Chopin's brilliant treatment of the piano, showing off the many innate characteristics and facets of the instrument, that have kept this music alive.

The Concerto No. 1 opens, naturally, with the orchestra, which lays out the musical material to be developed later by the piano. This was a standard approach for the first movement of a concerto, but here it only seems to enhance and spotlight the piano's first entry. The second movement is a Romance, where the orchestra is given even less to do. It again opens the movement, this time with muted strings, but then leaves the piano all alone for its entrance. After this, not much happens, but it's not so much what doesn't happen, as much as how it happens that is the point of Chopin's approach. He continually ornaments and embroiders the main tune, creating a movement of great serenity and calm. He wrote to a friend, "It is intended to convey the impression which one receives when the eye rests on a beloved landscape that calls up in one's soul beautiful memories, like on a fine moonlit spring evening." In the finale, Chopin introduces the strong Polish element of a folk dance known as a *krakowiak*, originating in the Krakow region.

The Italian pianist Maurizio Pollini is one of today's great interpreters of Chopin. In 1960, at the age of eighteen, Pollini walked away with the first prize in the Chopin International Piano Competition in Warsaw. The great Chopin pianist of the previous generation, Artur Rubinstein, was on the jury and said, "Pollini showed a complete supremacy over the others." Pollini had played the Piano Concerto No. 1 by Chopin in the final round of the competition, and shortly after his win this recording was made. He has all the traits of a great Chopin pianist: a brilliant, clean technique, with flexible phrasing and passion, and the recording captures the essential singing quality of the piano that never stoops to sentimentality. The additional solo items included are just as refined, taken from Pollini's first EMI solo recital recording.

FRÉDÉRIC CHOPIN: *Piano Concerto No. 1, Op. 11, etc.*
Maurizio Pollini, Philharmonia Orchestra/Paul Kletzki
EMI Classics 567 549-2

FRÉDÉRIC CHOPIN (1810–1849):
Waltzes

The word *waltz* usually paints the image of a huge ballroom, hooped skirts, and hundreds of people dancing in Vienna sometime during the second half of the nineteenth century. It was Vienna's Golden Age, with the Hapsburg Empire at its height and the music of the Waltz King, Johann Strauss, Jr., capturing the confidence and flair of the city. There are few for whom the titles "The Beautiful Blue Danube," "Tales from the Vienna Woods," or "Vienna Blood" don't conjure up the swirling sweep of the Viennese waltz at its finest. But there is another kind of waltz – those written for piano by Frédéric Chopin.

Chopin was Polish-born and spent only a little time in Vienna in the early part of his career, before settling in Paris. At the time, the Viennese waltz was just getting started, with those by Josef Lanner and Johann Strauss, Sr. – the father of the Waltz King. Later, Chopin claimed that very little of Viennese culture had stayed with him, saying, "The Viennese waltz is not for me." He never intended his waltzes to be danced. They were for listening, or as one music critic once described them, "They are dances for the soul, not for the body."

In his waltzes, Chopin created wonderful examples of salon music – elegant, refined, polished and expressive, more of Paris than Vienna. They tend to fall into two styles – bright and brilliant, or pensive and melancholic. Probably the most famous are the Op. 18 Grande Valse Brillante, the "Minute" Waltz, Op. 64, No. 1, and the Waltz in C Sharp Minor, Op. 64, No. 2. The "Minute" Waltz was never intended to be played in sixty seconds, as is sometimes believed, and attempted. The nickname probably comes from the French word for small, and had nothing to do with timespan. These, and the other waltzes by Chopin, have become some of the world's most-loved music for solo piano. The name Artur Rubinstein is inextricably linked with the music of Chopin. His Polish birth may have something to do with it. His warm, extroverted personality may be another reason. But regardless of the reason, Rubinstein's Chopin is a sure thing. It's direct, not fussy or sentimentalized, with a large tone, giving the music a lyrical warmth that is spontaneous and fresh. Rubinstein once claimed that he was the happiest man he ever met, and that love of life and music came across in everything he recorded, including almost all of the piano music composed by Chopin. He loved the piano and its music, and every emotion and mood is sincere. Before the public's eyes and ears until the age of ninety, Rubinstein never lost his joie de vivre and played like a young man throughout his long career. He died in 1982 at the age of ninety-five.

■───

FRÉDÉRIC CHOPIN: *Waltzes*
Artur Rubinstein
RCA Victor Red Seal   09026-63047-2

FRANZ LISZT (1811–1886):
Six Grandes Études de Paganini

Franz Liszt almost invented the piano virtuoso. At the peak of his fame in the nineteenth century, no other performer could brag of the kind of hero worship that Liszt received wherever he played. Tall and handsome with a glorious mane of hair, he was a born showman. Women fainted when he appeared from the wings and fought over his discarded cigar butts. Like a great actor, Liszt used facial contortions, hair tosses, and a lot of bobbing and weaving at the piano keyboard to enrapture his audiences. He had a great sense of style, enhanced by theatrics, even hysterics, and there was no end to his dramatizing, of both himself and his performance. One eyewitness described a Liszt recital:

> As the closing strains began, I saw Liszt's countenance assume that agony of expression, mingled with radiant smiles of joy, which I never saw in any other human face except in the paintings of our Saviour by some early masters. He fainted in the arms of a friend, and we bore him out in a fit of hysterics. The whole room sat breathless with fear, until the friend came forward and announced that Liszt had been restored to consciousness and was comparatively well again.

Liszt originated the piano recital – the first composer to dare to present an entire concert solo, without the usual added attractions of other artists or an orchestra. And he was the first pianist to perform in profile. Previously, the concert pianist had either faced the audience, or had his back to it. Well aware of his handsome profile and eager to use it to full advantage, Liszt turned the piano to best suit his appearance.

Liszt had learned his trade from another musical master – the great violinist Nicolò Paganini (1782–1840). In 1832, the twenty-year-old Liszt heard Paganini play in Paris, and the effect the performance had on him never left him. Paganini's astonishing mastery of his instrument, combined with an almost hypnotic onstage dramatic power mesmerized audiences. Liszt wrote to a friend, "What a man, what a violinist, what an artist! What sufferings, what misery, what tortures in those four strings!"

Liszt was already renowned at the time for a blistering technique, but now he realized that technique combined with wizardry and drama was what was required. He decided to become the Paganini of the piano. For two years, Liszt dove into the complete mastery of piano technique. He also read voraciously – Homer, the Bible, Plato, Shakespeare, and Byron. He wrote to a friend, "Unless I go mad, you will find an artist in me."

The six *Études d'exécution transcendante d'après Paganini* by Liszt were published in 1838 and are often considered the birth of keyboard virtuosity. In 1851, he revised the études and called them simply *Grandes Études de Paganini*, and it's this later version that's featured on the recommended recording. Five of the six Paganini *Études* by Liszt are based on the Twenty-Four Caprices for solo violin by Paganini – a tour de force of violin technique and flair. Only the Etude No. 3 is based on other music by Paganini: the finale of the Violin Concerto No. 2.

Canadian pianist Marc-André Hamelin owns one of the most impressive techniques of any pianist working today. There doesn't seem to be anything, by anyone, that can faze him. As it should, the music comes across as effortless. The pianist cannot be seen or heard to be struggling, or much of the Liszt effect is lost. Hamelin's cool confidence, security, and flair clearly illustrate the legacy of Franz Liszt.

FRANZ LISZT: *Six Grandes Études de Paganini*
Marc-André Hamelin
Hyperion   CDA67370

RICHARD WAGNER (1813–1883):
Opera Excerpts & Highlights

Opera in the second half of the nineteenth century was dominated by two men: Giuseppe Verdi in Italy and Richard Wagner in Germany. Both had come to opera with limited musical training, as both were largely self-taught, but both developed into consummate professionals in their chosen art. And of all the great composers, Wagner was one of the latest bloomers.

He came from a modest background, but a love for the theatre was evident very early. Wagner had showed considerable talents as a young writer, writing a Shakespearean-like tragedy while still a teenager. He also showed some promise in music, but was mostly impatient and apathetic. Gradually his tastes turned to opera, and the combining of music with the theatre opened up to him a whole new, powerful medium in which human experience and emotions could be conveyed with vivid characterization and rich insight.

After a few early, unsuccessful operas, Wagner wrote the music and libretto for *Der Fliegende Holländer* or *The Flying Dutchman*, the story of a sea captain doomed to roam the seven seas in search of a woman who would love him faithfully. This theme of redemption occurs again and again in the works of Wagner. *Dutchman* was only moderately successful, but it established Wagner as a composer of worth and launched his career. He would continue to be involved in all aspects of opera production – from libretto to music, to conducting, set design, and stage direction.

With Tannhäuser and Lohengrin, Wagner continued the theme of redemption and broadened the scope of opera forever.

Instead of set pieces and individual numbers, the action and music were continuous and seamless. And he further developed the concept of the leitmotif. This compositional tool, in which a theme can be assigned to the various characters, objects, or ideas, became the backbone of Wagner's music dramas. By altering or developing the leitmotif, the composer can comment on or suggest what's happening in the story. Wagner wove each leitmotif, sometimes hundreds of them, into the rich musical fabric of each opera.

In the 1850s, Wagner turned to his most ambitious work, and one that would occupy him, off and on, for a quarter of a century. *The Ring of the Nibelung*, a four-opera cycle that concludes with the destruction of the world by fire, represented many of the sociopolitical conditions in Europe at the time, and the theme of redemption through love, and death, appears yet again.

The composition of the Ring cycle was interrupted for *Tristan und Isolde*, which premiered in 1865. Here Wagner used a rich continuous style of unresolved music to powerfully depict the longing and frustration of the two doomed lovers. Only in the final scene, the *Liebestod*, when Tristan and Isolde are finally united in death, does the music resolve.

Die Meistersinger von Nürnberg, Wagner's only comedy, also dates from the 1860s. The music here is warmer and more good-humoured. The story tells of a noble poet-musician who, by his victory in a singing contest, wins fame and fortune as well as the hand of his beloved.

In 1876, Wagner's dream of a special festival opera house for performances of the four operas of his Ring cycle came true. "Mad" King Ludwig II of Bavaria, long a Wagner devotee and financial backer, came up with the needed funds, and the Bayreuth Festival was born. It continues to the present day, staging all of Wagner's works.

Parsifal, his final music drama, was premiered at Bayreuth in 1882. It again focuses on the theme of redemption, but here it's achieved through renunciation and compassion. Wagner died the following year in Venice. His body was brought back to Bayreuth for burial.

Few composers in history have had the impact of Wagner. Not only did he change music itself, but he changed the use and perception of it. In his works, Wagner used a new, sensual music, altering the use of melody, harmony, voice, and orchestra forever.

This recommended recording contains excerpts from most of the music dramas by Wagner, taken from legendary recordings over the last forty years. Singers such as Birgit Nilsson, Dietrich Fischer-Dieskau, and Placido Domingo are teamed with such famous Wagner conductors as Karl Böhm and Eugen Jochum for a highly satisfying cross-section of Wagner's art.

■

RICHARD WAGNER: *Opera Excerpts & Highlights*
A variety of soloists, orchestras and conductors
DGG Panorama   469 226-2

GIUSEPPE VERDI (1813–1901):
Opera Excerpts & Highlights

The Italians loved and identified with opera so much that some of Italy's composers devoted almost all their efforts to its composition, to the exclusion of symphonies, chamber music, and other genres. But few of them rose to the heights or had the skills of Giuseppe Verdi.

Verdi had received a sketchy musical education. By the time he was twenty, he had enough knowledge and skill for rural music positions, but he was refused entry into the Milan Conservatory. He was not a good pianist, and his grasp of music theory and composition was weak. But determined, he nevertheless composed an opera titled *Oberto* in the 1830s, and it was successfully staged at La Scala in Milan in 1839. The success led to commissions, one of which was *Nabucco*, produced for La Scala in 1842. With *Nabucco*, opera lovers quickly realized that a fresh voice in Italian opera had arrived. Verdi expanded upon what his *bel canto* predecessors Donizetti, Bellini, and Rossini had achieved. The orchestra was now larger and stronger, and the music moved with a clearer direction and momentum. In *bel canto*, a fair amount of time was given over to the leads for purely vocal pyrotechnics and display. The audiences loved it. But with Verdi, although the display remained, it now served the opera, and not vice versa. It was there for the purpose of expressing emotion, not for mere artist bravura and exhibitionism.

Verdi was a keen Italian nationalist, and the success of *Nabucco* made him not just a composer but a political figure, as well. At the time, Italy was under Austrian rule. There was the hope of a united

Italy under its own rule one day, and one of the choruses from *Nabucco* fed fuel to the nationalist fire. In the opera, the chorus number "Va, pensiero" tells of the Hebrew slaves' longing for their homeland. It's doubtful that Verdi intended the chorus to have political resonance for its audiences, but that's what happened. *Nabucco* and Verdi became symbols of the Italian resistance, and an acronym was made from his surname that represented the drive for the unification of Italy under one king: "Vittorio Emmanuele, Re d'Italia."

In the 1850s, Verdi reached his maturity with *Rigoletto, Il Trovatore* and *La Traviata*. They made his name a household word, and he became one of the most successful and popular opera composers in the world. Verdi, the great dramatist, was now in full sail. The smooth *bel canto* traits, which concentrated on a beauty of sound, had been traded in for a tougher kind of music that better suited the characters and the stories. The emotions and intensity had grown considerably into, really, a new kind of opera, sometimes described as "blood and thunder."

By the 1870s, Verdi was Italy's greatest composer, after a string of successes that included *Don Carlo, La Forza del Destino* and *Aida* among them. He went into a form of retirement for several years, basking in his fame and glory. But in his seventies, the plays of Shakespeare spurred him to return to composition, writing his greatest tragedy, *Otello*, in 1887. Because of an early failure, Verdi had avoided comedies through the bulk of his career. But in 1893, *Falstaff* was produced in Milan to great acclaim. It was to be his last opera. Verdi had long had plans for an operatic setting of *King Lear* by Shakespeare, but they remained unfulfilled. He died in 1901 at the age of eighty-seven.

This two-CD set of excerpts from some of Verdi's operas includes selections from *Nabucco, La Traviata, Rigoletto, La Forza del Destino, Il Trovatore,* and *Aida*. It features top Verdi singers, like Ileana Cotrubas, Placido Domingo, Carlo Bergonzi, Renata Scotto, and José Carreras, and the great Verdi conductors Tullio

Serafin, Carlos Kleiber, and Claudio Abbado, among others. It's a very strong selection of the works of this most important of nineteenth-century Italian composers.

■ _____

GIUSEPPE VERDI: *Opera Excerpts & Highlights*
A variety of soloists, orchestras, and conductors
DGG Panorama 469 217-2

CÉSAR FRANCK (1822–1890):
Violin Sonata in A

There are many cases of child prodigies throughout music history. Mozart, Beethoven, Schubert, Mendelssohn, and Korngold were all very talented in their youth, showing a musical maturity way beyond their years. But early success can sometimes result in burnout. And for some, once the novelty of child prodigy wears off, a void takes its place. Mozart, for example, never found the permanent job he longed for as an adult, after being the darling of European society as a child. Schubert too never found secure employment as a musician. He had composed brilliant, well-crafted songs as a teenager, but died penniless at the age of thirty-one.

The Belgian-born French musician César Franck suffered the reverse fate. He didn't experience public success as a composer until he was in his late sixties. Part of the reason was musical politics at the time in Paris, where Franck was based. Part of it was because he was an organist and organ teacher for much of his professional career. No one took him seriously, except as a composer of organ music. And part of Franck's lack of success lay in his character. He was a quiet, quaint man, modest, shy, and absent-minded. He never hawked his compositions, he never hustled for jobs. He was a simple man who served music and God with humility and reverence, and was completely happy doing so. Franck's student, Claude Debussy, wrote of him, "The discovery of a beautiful harmony was sufficient to make him as happy as the day is long. This man who was unfortunate, unrecognized, possessed the soul of a child, and one so good that neither contradictory circumstances nor the wickedness of others could ever make him feel bitter. He served music without ever asking for renown."

Franck composed his Violin Sonata in A, his only sonata, in 1886 when he was sixty-three. It was intended as a wedding present for the violin virtuoso Eugène Ysaÿe, Franck's Belgian compatriot and friend. Ysaÿe received the score on his wedding day, learned it quickly, and performed it often in his recitals. The work caught on, and has been an important member of the violin repertoire ever since. Its popularity has led it to be transcribed for cello and flute, and it has become a valued member of the repertoire of those instruments, as well.

Franck loved the structure and architecture of music. It was one of his traits that other French musicians criticized, accusing Franck of selling out to German academicism. The sonata is cyclical, a form that Franck and other French composers enjoyed. In other words, the musical material of all four movements is derived from a single musical cell or building block. That cell is heard right at the start on the violin, after a short piano introduction. Then it reappears in subsequent movements, in any number of different characterizations and contexts. Franck saves the best for the last movement, where the treatment of the musical cell is most complex. Here he uses canonic form, in which both violin and piano feature another variation of the cell, but starting at different times.

The Decca recording of the Franck Sonata with violinist Kyung-Wha Chung and pianist Radu Lupu has been a favourite ever since its initial release in the late 1970s. Chung and Lupu give the work a warm, passionate reading, never overdone. The French elegance of the sonata, the clarity and detail of line and texture, are closely observed in a natural, unforced style. This recording has always been considered a classic, and shows no signs of ever giving up that status.

CÉSAR FRANCK: *Violin Sonata in A*

Kyung-Wha Chung, Radu Lupu

Decca   421 154-2

ANTON BRUCKNER (1824–1896):
Symphony No. 4 in E-flat, "Romantic"

One of the most insecure composers was Anton Bruckner. He came from rural Austria, and spent the early part of his career as a village organist and choirmaster. And his lack of confidence stemmed largely from this background. In 1868 he moved to the bustling, cosmopolitan centre of Vienna to take up a teaching position and he remained there for the rest of his life. But to the cultured and snobby Viennese, Bruckner was always the hayseed, the country bumpkin. He suffered constant ridicule and harsh criticism, especially from the influential Viennese music critic Eduard Hanslick.

During rehearsals for the premiere of Bruckner's Symphony No. 4, the conductor, puzzled, stopped at one point, turned to Bruckner, and asked him, "What note is this?" Bruckner, ever wanting to please, quickly answered, "Any note you choose. Quite as you like." Then, when the rehearsal was over, Bruckner approached the conductor, pressed a small coin into his hand and said, "Take this and drink a stein of beer to my health." The conductor was shocked, but kept the coin so as not to offend the composer.

Bruckner's insecurity and desire to please resulted in continual revisions and alterations of his works. For example, he composed the Symphony No. 4 in 1874, but it was not performed. Several years later, he reworked the symphony, adding a completely new third movement and revising the finale. It was in this form that the work was premiered in Vienna in 1881. Bruckner continued to revise and change it though, and in 1889 when he was readying the

Fourth for publication, well-meaning friends, whose admiration for him did not match their understanding of his music, advised him to rework it further, making severe cuts and re-orchestrations. Long after his death, in 1936, the International Bruckner Society published the Symphony No. 4 in the version that had been used for the 1881 Viennese premiere, edited by Robert Haas. Then in 1953, another performing edition appeared, by the Austrian musicologist and Bruckner scholar, Leopold Nowak. The consensus today is that Bruckner's initial plans for his works were the closest to his intentions, and that he was led off-track by his friends and editors.

The subtitle of the Symphony No. 4 is "Romantic," and was likely attached by Bruckner himself, but again, at the urging of friends. He even went so far as to attach a program, which has probably done more harm than good. His friends may have felt that a romantic storyline of medieval castles, with knights, ladies-in-waiting, hunts, and lavish feasts would increase interest in the symphony. It's pretty obvious that Bruckner himself was not completely convinced since, at one point, he admitted he couldn't even remember what the storyline was for the finale. These half-baked, contrived ideas only added to the general view of Bruckner as the country bumpkin – a naive, innocent composer with some talent, but little intellectual depth. Since the end of the Second World War, Bruckner's music has grown in popularity and today it has gained the recognition it deserves.

Austrian conductor Karl Böhm seemed to realize that the essence of Bruckner was to be found in the original versions of his works and not in the revisions. As early as the 1930s, Böhm was performing and recording Bruckner uncut, making the case for allowing the music to speak for itself. By the time he made this recording in 1973, Böhm had been conducting the Bruckner symphonies for almost fifty years. It's a spacious, majestic reading, stressing the lyrical aspects with flexible and shapely phrasing.

ANTON BRUCKNER: *Symphony No. 4 in E-flat, "Romantic"*
Vienna Philharmonic Orchestra/Karl Böhm
Decca Legends   466 374-2

JOHANN STRAUSS, JR. (1825–1899): *Waltzes*

Johann Strauss, Jr., commonly known as "the Waltz King," came to his profession naturally. His father, Johann Strauss, Sr., was a member of the dance orchestra of Josef Lanner before starting up his own highly successful ensemble in Vienna in the 1820s. The elder Strauss enjoyed a bustling international career, but discouraged his sons from following in his footsteps. The first son, Johann, Jr., disobeyed, establishing his own orchestra in Vienna, in competition with his father. Father and son eventually reconciled, and on the father's death in 1849, Johann, Jr., took over the direction of both orchestras, and amalgamated them. Vienna was so crazy for waltz music at the time, and Johann, Jr., was so good at filling the demand for it, that he eventually had six orchestras in Vienna, and every night he flitted from one to the other, making a brief appearance at each. Right up until his death in 1899, Strauss, Jr., conducted and toured with his orchestra, and composed hundreds of waltzes, polkas, and other dances.

The Viennese waltz craze peaked in the 1850s and '60s. Strauss compositions like the "Blue Danube," "Roses from the South," "Emperor Waltz," and "Tales from the Vienna Woods" are some of the most popular waltzes ever penned and today symbolize the Golden Age of Vienna, when it was the political, scientific, and artistic hub of Europe in the second half of the nineteenth century.

The origins of the waltz have always been sketchy, but it's believed to have evolved out of the *Ländler*, an Austrian peasant dance in triple time (three beats to a bar). It's ironic that, at first, the somewhat snobby Viennese viewed the Ländler as too coarse and crude for their cultured and civilized tastes. Even by mid-century, some of the more prudish found its swirling character and the embrace of the dancers to be a little too "familiar." In earlier dances, minuets and gavottes, for instance, the two dancers barely touched fingertips.

As the waltz fad grew, it spread from the ballrooms and dance halls of Vienna to cafés, theatres, and people's homes. On one visit to Vienna, composer Richard Wagner remarked that the waltz "was a stronger narcotic than alcohol." Some serious music critics began to worry that Vienna was dumbing-down and becoming incapable of "intellectual exertion." Johannes Brahms, a friend and admirer of the Waltz King, once autographed a woman's fan with the opening bars of the "Blue Danube" and signed it, "Unfortunately not by J. Brahms." In the hands of the Waltz King, waltz combined brilliance, sentiment, sparkle, and nostalgia and became the musical metaphor of a glorious, sophisticated society at its peak.

You just can't beat Willi Boskovsky in this repertoire. He was born, raised, and educated in Vienna, and spent most of his career as violin leader of the Vienna Philharmonic Orchestra. Boskovsky continued the tradition of the Strauss family by directing with his violin bow while playing, and he led the famous New Year's Day Concert from Vienna for twenty-five years. Boskovsky achieved an old-world elegance in the waltz. His lilting way with tempos and rhythms, the shapely phrasing, and never forgetting the dance origins of this music, make these accounts sophisticated, sensual, and satisfying.

■ ──

JOHANN STRAUSS, JR.: *Waltzes*
Vienna Philharmonic Orchestra/Willi Boskovsky
Decca Eloquence 467 413-2

JOHANNES BRAHMS (1833–1897): *Symphony No. 2 in D, Op. 73*

As did many other composers after Beethoven, Johannes Brahms felt terribly insecure, at first, in the realm of the symphony. He admired and respected Beethoven "Nine" so much that he wrote, "You have no idea how people like me feel when we hear the footsteps of a giant like him behind us."

As a result of this fear of not measuring up to Beethoven, it took Brahms over twenty years of hard work to feel confident enough to have his Symphony No. 1 publicly performed. And, of course, when it was finally premiered in 1876, it was the links to the works of Beethoven that the critics and public noticed. But he was over the hurdle; his fear had been conquered. It must have been somewhat of a relief, then, for him to begin work on the Symphony No. 2 right away. He finished it in a mere four months, compared to the two decades it took to complete No. 1. The new symphony debuted in 1877, only one year after the Symphony No. 1.

Throughout his career, Brahms tended to be modest, evasive, and even flippant about his own music when questioned by friends. Regarding the Symphony No. 2, he wrote to a friend, "Don't expect anything special. It's nothing but a tiny, innocent piece." (The Symphony No. 2 is Brahms's most richly orchestrated symphony and a good forty-five to fifty minutes in length.) To another friend, he wrote, "I do not know whether I have a pretty symphony. I must enquire of skilled persons."

The Symphony No. 2 is his warmest and most lyrical, and it's sometimes called his "sunny" symphony or his "pastorale." Typical of Brahms, there are still sections of drama and stress, but by the time we reach the finale, we are carried along with stirring, vigorous, and victorious music. Much of the musical material of all four movements is based on the three-note motif heard at the very beginning (D, C-sharp, D).

The Academic Festival Overture is a tribute to university life, and includes several student drinking songs. Brahms composed it for the University of Breslau when that institution awarded him an honorary degree in 1879.

Claudio Abbado recorded a complete Brahms Symphony cycle with the Berlin Philharmonic after he became artistic director of the famed orchestra, following the death of his predecessor, Herbert von Karajan, in 1989. Even in these early days, Abbado was making his stamp, and the orchestra plays beautifully for him. Where Karajan had achieved a highly refined and seamless orchestral sound, Abbado strived for, and got, a sound that was a little lighter and in which the sections of the orchestra were more clearly delineated. Abbado's Brahms is old school – big, lush, warm, and passionate. Things never get bogged down, he never loses sight of the overall picture, and he makes the most of Brahms's play of tension and release in the music.

■ ──────────────────────────────

JOHANNES BRAHMS: *Symphony No. 2 in D, Op. 73*
  & Academic Festival Overture
Berlin Philharmonic Orchestra/Claudio Abbado
DGG Eloquence   469 685-2

JOHANNES BRAHMS (1833–1897):
Ein Deutsches Requiem (A German Requiem), Op. 45

Brahms had come from northern Germany and a Protestant, not Roman Catholic, background. But he was never an overly religious man, and remained unconvinced of the Christian belief in resurrection and life after death. After the death of his friend and mentor Robert Schumann in 1856, Brahms began to think of composing a requiem. It's possible that Schumann himself had intended to write a requiem, and that Brahms wanted to fulfill Schumann's dream. It is unusual for a composer at the young age of twenty-three to contemplate writing a requiem.

Then, in 1865, Brahms's mother died, and he again turned to thoughts of a requiem. By 1866, he had completed a six-movement work and had it performed. Not completely satisfied, Brahms then added another movement, and it's this final seven-movement version that has come to be known and loved around the globe. It was Brahms's first big success, and the one that made his name internationally.

Roman Catholic requiem masses had been composed for centuries, and usually dealt with Judgment Day, the payment for sins, the fear and terror of damnation, and the praying for the souls of the dead. These concepts worked against Brahms's own views and personal beliefs, so instead of setting the standard text, the Latin Mass for the Dead, Brahms compiled his own, chosen from the German translation of the Bible by Martin Luther. He called the work *Ein Deutsches Requiem*, or *A German Requiem*, although he later claimed, "As regards the title, I could easily have left out 'German' and substituted 'Human.' "

The *German Requiem* by Brahms is more optimistic than other requiems, conveying hope and consolation, rather than despair and fear. It's a work that deals with comforting the living, and a resigned acceptance of death, instead of begging forgiveness for the dead. Where the Latin Requiem Mass begins with a plea for eternal rest for the dead, the Brahms *Requiem* begins with one of the Beatitudes: "Blessed are they that mourn, for they shall be comforted." The living instead of the dead.

Otto Klemperer's recording of the Brahms *Requiem* has been famous ever since it was made in 1961. There's a solid, rugged, confident quality to it, with exceptional playing and singing from the Philharmonia Orchestra & Chorus, in their heyday, and some exquisite performing from the two soloists, soprano Elisabeth Schwarzkopf and baritone Dietrich Fischer-Dieskau. Compared to other recordings of the work, this one presents Brahms's intentions the best. It's warm, emotional, spiritual, and expressive, and convincingly "human."

■ ————————————————

JOHANNES BRAHMS: *Ein Deutsches Requiem, Op. 45*
Elisabeth Schwarzkopf, Dietrich Fischer-Dieskau,
    Philharmonia Orchestra & Chorus/Otto Klemperer
EMI Classics   CDM 566 903-2

JOHANNES BRAHMS (1833–1897):
Violin Concerto in D, Op. 77

Brahms had been trained as a pianist as a boy and he developed into quite a talented one. For a while, he was on the path to becoming a virtuoso pianist, before composing took over and he changed his focus. Brahms was a severe critic of his own music, and often turned to his musical friends for their comments and reactions on his compositions. So when Brahms began to compose his one and only violin concerto in 1878, he naturally turned for advice to his trusted friend, the great violinist Joseph Joachim. Brahms sought Joachim's input several times. At first, he sent Joachim the solo part, requesting that he mark the passages difficult, awkward, or impossible. Joachim complied and added fingering and bowing indications. The premiere took place in Leipzig on New Year's Day, 1879, with Joachim as soloist and Brahms conducting. But after the premiere, Brahms still had misgivings. He wrote to Joachim, "I would be grateful for any alternative versions. Is the piece really good and practicable enough to be printed?" After a few more alterations, Brahms came around and realized the concerto was a strong one, writing to his publisher, "It is well to be doubted whether I could write a better concerto." The Viennese music critic Eduard Hanslick referred to the work as "the ripe fruit of the friendship between Joachim and Brahms."

But how much of Joachim's advice Brahms actually followed has long been argued. Was it just the technical aspects, like fingerings and bowing marks? Or did Joachim, a composer himself, offer musical and structural suggestions and solutions? And if so, how many of these did Brahms incorporate? We will probably never know, for the work is Brahmsian to the core, and sounds as if it was composed easily in a single spurt of inspiration.

Joachim's performance style concentrated on musical integrity and lyricism rather than virtuosity, and the Brahms Violin Concerto reflects this. Like the Beethoven Violin Concerto, the violin and orchestra are closely knit together into one fabric. And, although difficult to play, the Brahms Concerto never displays virtuosity for its own sake. "Latent heat behind formal exterior" was a phrase once used to describe Brahms's music, and it works very well for the violin concerto.

The overall lyrical qualities of the concerto are announced right at the start of the huge first movement by the orchestral introduction. It overflows with musical ideas, before the solo violin enters, adding drama and passion. The slow second movement is a kind of hybrid of a lullaby and a hymn. In the extended introduction for winds, the oboe states the main musical idea, which is taken up and embroidered by the solo violin. For the finale, Brahms changes gears completely with a robust Hungarian and gypsy-inspired folk dance. Joseph Joachim was Hungarian-born, and Brahms may have been doffing his hat to his friend and confidant.

The Siberian-born violinist Maxim Vengerov had wowed audiences with his white-hot interpretations of some of the Russian violin concerto repertoire before he made this live concert recording of the Brahms Concerto in Chicago in 1997. Playing before an audience brought a tension and excitement to the orchestra and soloist that only enhances their performance. Vengerov, in a technically brilliant reading, beautifully balances the stocky, hearty side of Brahms with the tender and lyrical.

■─────────────────────────────────────

JOHANNES BRAHMS: *Violin Concerto in D, Op.* 77
Maxim Vengerov, Chicago Symphony Orchestra/Daniel Barenboim
Teldec 0630-17144-2

JOHANNES BRAHMS (1833–1897):
Piano Concertos Nos. 1 & 2

The nineteenth-century concerto was often used as a vehicle to exhibit the brilliant talents of the performer. It puts the soloist in the spotlight and makes him or her a hero. But Brahms had little interest in music designed to show off the talents of the performer. He was much more interested in the music as a language of communication, and was therefore labelled an esoteric conservative by many of his contemporaries. He avoided all virtuoso trappings in his concertos, and strove to make them more symphonic – more of a mix of concerto and symphony – a symphony that happened to also feature a solo instrument, and put both solo instrument and orchestra on equal ground. Tchaikovsky never understood the music of Brahms and once called him "a giftless bastard."

Brahms's Piano Concerto No. 1 was completed in 1858. Originally conceived as his first symphony, the concerto does contain the grandeur and scope of a symphony. Two decades later, Brahms composed the Piano Concerto No. 2. It's longer than the first and contains four movements instead of three – unusual for a concerto, but the norm for a symphony. And yet in both concertos, the full forces are rarely called upon. Brahms writes in an almost chamber music style, often pairing only a handful of instruments with the piano.

The Piano Concerto No. 1 begins darkly and tragically, a great example of a young Romantic composer spreading his wings. Some speculate that this music represented Brahms's anger and despair at the death of his friend and mentor, Robert Schumann, in 1856. It was probably this austere opening that turned early audiences off this concerto. Gradually the darkness lifts, though, and we are presented with a number of more lyrical ideas, some introduced by the orchestra, some by the piano. On the original manuscript of the second movement, Brahms wrote "Benedictus Qui Venit in Nomine Domini" ("Blessed is he who cometh in the name of the Lord") – believed to be another reference to the memory of Robert Schumann. The finale begins as a stocky march, but with softer, more gentle interludes, capping it all off with a brilliant ending.

Over twenty years passed before Brahms completed the Piano Concerto No. 2. It's on an even grander scale than the First, but once again, Brahms downplayed his accomplishment, modestly writing to a friend, "I have written a tiny, tiny piano concerto." Furthering his desire to blend the concerto form with the symphonic, Brahms assigns the musical material in the first movement equally to the pianist and the orchestra. He described the second movement as a "tiny, tiny wisp of a Scherzo," but some of the most passionate and dramatic music in the work is here. The third movement is a soulful song with extended solo passages for cello, and the gentle character continues into the finale, where it's mixed with passion and ardour.

The Soviet pianist Emil Gilels was one of the great interpreters of the piano music of Brahms in the twentieth century. His playing could be bold, hearty, and stocky, but also warm and compelling – lending itself exceptionally well to Brahms. Overall, what comes across here are majestic readings, a rich piano tone, and a good balance.

■

JOHANNES BRAHMS: *Piano Concertos Nos. 1 & 2*
Emil Gilels, Berlin Philharmonic Orchestra/Eugen Jochum
DGG The Originals   447 446-2

JOHANNES BRAHMS (1833–1897):
Solo Piano Music

Like Mozart, Beethoven, Chopin, and Liszt, Brahms in his youth was a gifted pianist. As he grew older and developed more and more into a composer, his pianistic skills waned, but he always showed a deep love and comfort in writing for solo piano. And yet, despite this interest, Brahms's output for solo piano is limited. His three piano sonatas were all composed by the time he turned twenty. In the middle part of his career, he turned to sets of variations, as well as to some shorter pieces. Then late in life, Brahms returned to the piano and created four collections of short piano works with vague titles like "Capriccio," "Intermezzo," "Ballade," and "Rhapsody."

These late piano works that make up his Op. 116, 117, 118, and 119 are among Brahms's finest creations, and some of his most personal. Their short length can sometimes fool one into thinking that they are inconsequential, but nothing could be further from the truth. In these short pieces, Brahms has successfully focused and concentrated his ideas. The great pianist Artur Rubinstein wrote of them, "Brahms in his final years produced serene and nostalgic music that was ever more inward in mood. As his own notations in the score indicate, they are so intensely intimate that one cannot really convey their full substance to a large audience. They should be heard quietly, in a small room, for they are actually works of chamber music for the piano."

Many music lovers in Vienna during the 1890s found these "late" piano pieces by Brahms a little too modern. And there's no doubt that Brahms was experimenting with the use of dissonance, harmony, and expression. Maybe that's why the next generation of composers, among them Arnold Schoenberg and Alexander Zemlinsky, held these pieces in such high esteem. They are often described as "bittersweet," "autumnal," "nostalgic," or "yearning." However you describe them, they are unmistakably Brahms, and make the perfect summation of his life and career.

The Rumanian-born, Russian-trained pianist Radu Lupu is one of the great Brahms pianists, and this is one of his most popular recordings. He brings to these works a serene, spiritual sheen and a quiet emotional intensity that can't fail to move you. It's classic "late" Brahms, played as it should be.

■

JOHANNES BRAHMS: *Solo Piano Music*
Radu Lupu
Decca 417 599-2

CAMILLE SAINT-SAËNS (1835–1921): *The Carnival of the Animals*

The French composer Camille Saint-Saëns was yet another child prodigy, right up there with Mozart and Mendelssohn. By the age of five, he was composing songs and short piano pieces. By his early twenties, Saint-Saëns was recognized throughout Europe as a composer and brilliant performer on the organ and piano. He lived a long life that saw many changes in musical styles and tastes, but Saint-Saëns remained true to himself and consistent in his musical approach. As an old man, looking at some of his early compositions from when he was a child, he happily noted their correctness of form and technique. With a vast interest and knowledge of old music as well as contemporary, Saint-Saëns incorporated the best into his own. His music shows influences of sixteenth-century composers, through Beethoven, Liszt, Wagner, and Verdi. And in all of his music are the classic French traits of clarity, balance, proportion, and elegance. He once wrote, "The artist who does not feel completely satisfied by elegant lines, by harmonious colours, and by a beautiful succession of chords does not understand the art of music."

The Carnival of the Animals was composed in 1886, and subtitled "A Grand Zoological Fantasy." The composer regarded the work as a bit of a lark, a whim intended mainly for the enjoyment of a few of his friends. After a single private performance, Saint-Saëns refused to allow the work to be published or performed again in his lifetime. He was probably worried that the *Carnival*'s charm, wit, and accessibility would divert attention from his other, more serious works, such as the Symphony No. 3, composed in the same year. He was right. *The Carnival of the Animals* has become Saint-Saëns's most popular work. It was originally written for two pianos and a small instrumental ensemble. Saint-Saëns later orchestrated it, and decades later, the American poet Ogden Nash came up with verses to go along with the various animal depictions. The recommended recording is the original, chamber version and does not include the verses by Nash. Over fourteen sections, Saint-Saëns paints a menagerie of animals, from tortoises to elephants, from kangaroos to aquarium fish. He also quotes freely from other composers, usually with a wink of the eye. For example, the tortoises are heard in a lugubriously slow version of Offenbach's famous high-kicking cancan. The elephants dance to music from *The Damnation of Faust* by Berlioz, and Saint-Saëns even parodies himself. The xylophone knocks out his *Danse macabre* in "Fossils," and weaves it with strains from Rossini's *Barber of Seville* and two French folk songs. "The Swan" is the most beloved movement of the suite, and the only one Saint-Saëns allowed to be performed and published in his lifetime. The long, beautiful line of the cello melody evokes the majestic, gliding motions of a swan on water. "The Swan" took on a life of its own after the great Russian ballerina Anna Pavlova adopted it for one of her most famous solos.

Although light-hearted and often aimed at children, *The Carnival of the Animals* is a difficult piece, especially for the two pianists. This 2003 recording features a number of talented, young French musicians in a bubbling account. It's articulate, clean, bright, and witty, completely capturing the composer's intentions. These performers have a lot of fun performing together, and this enhances the enjoyment of the listener.

■ ─────────────────────────────────

CAMILLE SAINT-SAËNS: *The Carnival of the Animals*
Renaud Capuçon, Michel Dalberto, Emmanuel Pahud, and others
Virgin Classics   545 603-2

MAX BRUCH (1838–1920):
Violin Concertos Nos. 1 & 3

During his lifetime, the German composer Max Bruch was best known for his choral works, both sacred and secular. His oratorios *Moses* and *Arminius*, as well as the large-scale *Achilles* and *Odysseus* were highly regarded and performed often, making Bruch one of the most successful German Romantic composers. But musical tastes change, and today Bruch's fame rests mainly on a few works for solo stringed instruments with orchestra: the Violin Concerto No. 1, the Scottish Fantasy for Violin and Orchestra, and *Kol nidrei*, for cello and orchestra.

These concerted works by Bruch have become popular with soloists, conductors, and audiences alike because of their high craft. They showcase the virtuosic talents of the soloist and the solo instrument's full range of colours and sounds. But these works are also full of great melodies and passionate music. The great violin pedagogue and teacher of violinist Jascha Heifetz, Leopold Auer, summed up Bruch's talents nicely. Auer said, "The Bruch concertos occupy a position of honour in the violin repertoire. From the standpoint of the violinist who plays in public they are artistic Declarations of Independence; they are the eloquent and inspiring documents which supply the proof that Bruch freed himself from all mechanical fetters."

Bruch was not a violinist himself, although he had studied the instrument in his youth and learned to love it, referring to it once as "the queen of instruments." He began sketching his Violin Concerto No. 1 in 1857, and it was premiered in 1866. But Bruch was unhappy with the piece and soon began to revise it. He sent the score to his friend, Joseph Joachim, and asked for his advice, criticism, and suggestions. Joachim was the pre-eminent German violinist of the day, and was often asked for his opinions. A decade later, he helped Johannes Brahms with his violin concerto. Joachim made a number of suggestions to Bruch, and the new and improved version of the Violin Concerto No. 1 in G Minor was premiered publicly in 1868, with Joachim as the soloist and the dedicatee. It has become one of the most popular violin concertos in the repertoire.

Some twenty-five years later, Bruch composed his Violin Concerto No. 3. It was also dedicated to Joseph Joachim, who again supplied valuable advice and suggestions, and gave the premiere of the work in 1891. This one, unlike the first concerto, has not been able to secure a solid position in the standard repertoire. The reasons for its lack of popularity are cloudy. Like the first concerto, the third also has ample display for the soloist, great tunes, and passionate music. Its slow movement is every bit as attractive as its counterpart in the first concerto, if not more so.

The Canadian James Ehnes was a talented child violinist, winning many prizes and awards while still a teenager. He made his orchestral solo debut with the Montreal Symphony Orchestra at the age of thirteen. Ehnes's warm, sweet violin tone, shapely phrasing, and technical prowess are perfectly suited to these works by Bruch. The Montreal Symphony Orchestra under Charles Dutoit was famous for clarity and transparency in French orchestral music. Those attributes again work wonders here, in this German music, allowing James Ehnes to shine in a strong, collaborative recording.

■ ───

MAX BRUCH: *Violin Concertos Nos. 1 & 3*
James Ehnes, Orchestre Symphonique de Montréal/Charles Dutoit
CBC Records   SMCD 5207

MODEST MUSSORGSKY (1839–1881):
Pictures at an Exhibition

Modest Mussorgsky was one of the group of talented composers known as the "Russian Five" or "The Mighty Handful," the others being Mily Balakirev, Alexander Borodin, César Cui, and Nikolai Rimsky-Korsakov. Like his colleagues, Mussorgsky lacked any kind of formal musical education. He was trained for a career in the military. But the Russian Five's vision of establishing a truly Russian form of music helped them overcome their shortcomings to achieve their goal.

Mussorgsky was probably the most imaginative of the five, but his lack of proper musical training and confidence meant that many of his works were still incomplete by the time of his early death at forty-two in 1881. Several compositions were then completed by other Russian composers, especially his friend Rimsky-Korsakov. With the best of intentions, they reworked Mussorgsky's music, taking out many of the rough edges and smoothing over inconsistencies and discrepancies. In recent years, musicologists have gone back to the Mussorgsky originals, and opinions have changed. More and more today, it's believed that the bold ideas and rough-hewn nature of Mussorgsky's music are its strengths – not weaknesses. The other Russians, in their attempts to squeeze Mussorgsky into a mould, overlooked his creativity, originality, and vivid imagination.

In 1873, Victor Hartmann, the Russian painter, architect, and friend of Mussorgsky, died at the age of thirty-nine. A year later, a memorial exhibition of some of Hartmann's paintings, drawings, and sketches was put on in St. Petersburg. The show had such a powerful effect on Mussorgsky that he composed a piano work made up of musical depictions of ten of the Hartmann paintings. A promenade, in the tempo of a walk was used to preface and link some of the depictions. The result was one of the pinnacles of nineteenth-century piano repertoire – *Pictures at an Exhibition*. The work has sometimes been criticized for its lack of a suitable piano idiom, and some pianists, including Vladimir Horowitz, have made their own versions. There's even one for piano with orchestra. But again, the original version is the most powerful and original, bringing into focus Mussorgsky's own comment about his music: "With whatever shortcomings my music is born, with them it must live, if it is to live at all."

Pictures at an Exhibition developed another life in the twentieth century. Finally realizing its vivid imagination and worth, several musicians transcribed the work for orchestra, to employ the full range of orchestral colours and effects. In 1922, conductor Serge Koussevitzky commissioned Maurice Ravel to orchestrate *Pictures*, and it's this version that has become the most popular, with many people today unaware of the original piano version. Ravel was a master at orchestration, using the instruments like a painter uses colours, and he put his own distinct stamp on the work. His version remains true to the original, but expands and extends its scope as well as its effects.

This single recording features both the original solo piano version of *Pictures at an Exhibition* by Mussorgsky, as well as the Ravel orchestration, allowing listeners to make up their own minds about the values of each, and even to compare individual movements. Pianist Lazar Berman was trained in the traditions of the Russian piano school and brings an air of authority to the original piano score. Herbert von Karajan and the Berlin Philharmonic offer a magical account of Ravel's orchestration, electric in its intensity, that builds to the grand majesty of the final section, "The Great Gate of Kiev."

■ _____

MODEST MUSSORGSKY: *Pictures at an Exhibition*
   (original & Ravel orchestration)
Lazar Berman, piano
Berlin Philharmonic Orchestra/Herbert von Karajan
DGG Eloquence   469 626-2

PETER ILYICH TCHAIKOVSKY (1840–1893):
Piano Concerto No. 1 & Violin Concerto

At the midpoint of the nineteenth century, Russian music was dominated by two brothers. Anton Rubinstein enjoyed a stellar career as one of Europe's dazzling piano virtuosos before founding the St. Petersburg Conservatory in 1862. His younger brother, Nikolai, followed in Anton's footsteps, and established what became the Moscow Conservatory in 1864.

One of the reasons the Rubinsteins set up these first Russian music schools was to combat what they perceived as the low, unprofessional quality of music then being composed in Russia. Their training had been in the mainstream European style of music, where form, structure, and thematic development dominated.

At about the same time, a group of five Russian musicians banded together to try to establish a truly "Russian" brand of music, not based on the musical traditions of Germany, Italy, or France. Mily Balakirev, César Cui, Alexander Borodin, Modest Mussorgsky, and Nikolai Rimsky-Korsakov formed what became known as the "Russian Five" or the "Mighty Handful," to try to develop a Russian classical music that was based on Russian folk music, and told Russian stories about Russian people.

Peter Ilyich Tchaikovsky had been one of the first graduates of the St. Petersburg Conservatory. Trained in the Western European style, and especially fond of the music of Mozart, Tchaikovsky bridged the gap between the Rubinsteins and the "Five." His music, and maybe especially the concertos, is a wonderful blend of musical professionalism with national ancestry.

The Piano Concerto No. 1 by Tchaikovsky was composed in 1874 for Nikolai Rubinstein, the director of the Moscow Conservatory, where Tchaikovsky was working. Rubinstein hated the piece, describing it as trivial, derivative, and vulgar, and told Tchaikovsky to completely rewrite it. Tchaikovsky refused to change a single note, and instead rededicated the concerto to the German pianist Hans von Bülow, who thought it a powerful and original work. Von Bülow gave the premiere in Boston the following year, while on an American tour, and it is today one of the best-loved of all concertos. To his credit, Rubinstein later realized his mistake, entered the concerto into his repertoire, and performed it often. The main, sweeping melody of the first movement was adapted in the 1940s as the hit, "Tonight We Love."

A couple of years after the Piano Concerto No. 1, Tchaikovsky married one of his students to gain social acceptance and conceal his homosexuality. The marriage was short-lived and disastrous, and Tchaikovsky fled Russia, accompanied by his brother Modest. While he was away he composed his sole violin concerto, which he dedicated to the great violinist and teacher Leopold Auer. But, like Nikolai Rubinstein with the Piano Concerto No. 1, Auer disliked the work and refused to play it. So, once again, Tchaikovsky turned to someone else for the premiere, this time, Adolf Brodsky, who gave the first performance in Vienna in 1881. The prominent Viennese music critic at the time was Eduard Hanslick, who tended to hate anything Russian. In his review, Hanslick trashed the concerto, claiming it contained music "that stinks in the ear!" Like Nikolai Rubinstein before him, Leopold Auer too later ate his words, and came to appreciate the concerto. As he was no longer performing by that time, he championed the work by teaching it to his many students, including Nathan Milstein.

Pianist Martha Argerich has always performed the Piano Concerto No. 1 by Tchaikovsky as one of her party pieces. She's recorded it three times, and this, the first, is the finest. Not quite thirty years old at the time, Argerich brought a wide-eyed freshness to this over-played concerto, with a broad range of tonal colours, nicely matched by conductor Charles Dutoit and the Royal Philharmonic. It's a big, grand performance, with fire in the outer movements and a delicate soul-searching romanticism in the slow middle movement.

The Russian-born violinist Nathan Milstein studied with Leopold Auer, to whom the Tchaikovsky Violin Concerto was initially dedicated, and there is an authenticity to his recording. His playing is highly expressive, and the slow movement has the perfect degree of that particular brand of Russian melancholia and sensitivity. Conductor Claudio Abbado and the Vienna Philharmonic are well-balanced in their approach and very supportive.

■ ───────────────────────────────────

PETER ILYICH TCHAIKOVSKY: *Piano Concerto No. 1 &*
Violin Concerto
Martha Argerich, Nathan Milstein,
Royal Philharmonic Orchestra, Vienna Philharmonic Orchestra/
Charles Dutoit, Claudio Abbado
DGG   439 420-2

PETER ILYICH TCHAIKOVSKY (1840–1893):
Symphonies Nos. 4, 5, 6

One of the most sensitive and emotional of composers was the Russian Peter Ilyich Tchaikovsky. In his youth, Tchaikovsky was once described as a "porcelain" child. The slightest thing seemed to upset him, and any kind of criticism or reprimand would start the flow of tears. He remained hypersensitive throughout his life, and the fear of his homosexuality being discovered only added to his neurosis. And yet Tchaikovsky was a thoroughly professional composer, schooled in all the arts, well-read, and highly disciplined.

The Symphony No. 4 was composed after Tchaikovsky's brief but disastrous experience with marriage. In an effort to conceal his homosexuality, add some stability to his life, and enhance his professional stature, he married in 1877. It was a terrible mistake. He realized it immediately and tried to commit suicide. About the same time, he came into contact with one of the great benefactors in all music, Madame Nadezhda von Meck, to whom the Symphony No. 4 is dedicated. She provided Tchaikovsky with both financial and emotional support for a number of years, on the condition that they never meet or converse. The Symphony No. 4 is the first of his final three symphonies that deal with fate – "that tragic power which prevents the yearning for happiness from reaching its goal."

Tchaikovsky composed the Symphony No. 5 ten years later, and it too deals with the topic of fate, but more forcefully. Typically for Tchaikovsky, he had serious misgivings about the work and his talents as a composer. He wrote to his brother expressing worry that he was "written out," and confided in Madame von Meck that the Symphony No. 5 was a failure. But, as in the Fourth, by the finale, despair gives way to optimism, although now it's not as convincing, and we can't help but think Tchaikovsky is trying to put on a brave face.

It was Tchaikovsky's brother Modest who came up with the nickname "Pathétique" for the Symphony No. 6. The Russian meaning of the name suggests feelings of yearning and passion, rather than pathos or pity. Tchaikovsky had few doubts about this work, and believed it to be one of his best. In the Sixth, there is a musical depiction of a fierce internal psychological struggle, a coming to grips with one's fate. The symphony ends unusually, with a slow movement that's one of the darkest and most anguished in the repertoire, as if Tchaikovsky were saying goodbye to the world. It had a powerful effect on many composers who followed, including Mahler, Sibelius, Prokofiev, and Shostakovich. Tchaikovsky conducted the premiere of the Sixth in St. Petersburg in 1893. Nine days later he was dead.

Evgeny Mravinsky was the music director of the Leningrad Philharmonic Orchestra for fifty years. These recordings were made in London while the orchestra was on tour in 1960, and they've been legendary accounts ever since. At the time, no one had ever heard the Tchaikovsky symphonies played like this. They're driven, intense, and very Russian readings. The bright sections are hair-raising, while the melancholic passages plumb the dark depths of despair. Through them all courses the passion of Tchaikovsky and the Russian soul.

■

PETER ILYICH TCHAIKOVSKY: *Symphonies Nos. 4, 5, 6*
Leningrad Philharmonic Orchestra/Evgeny Mravinsky
DGG   419 745-2

PETER ILYICH TCHAIKOVSKY (1840–1893): *Ballet Suites*

Although Tchaikovsky composed a number of songs, piano pieces, and some chamber music, it was in the larger forms that his genius really thrived – opera, symphony, and ballet. He had a way of writing for an orchestra that was unique. Within seconds of hearing an orchestral work by Tchaikovsky, you can identify the composer. His sense of orchestration was brilliant and colourful.

This gift comes across especially in the three full-length ballets by Tchaikovsky – *Swan Lake*, *The Sleeping Beauty*, and *The Nutcracker*. Prior to Tchaikovsky, Russian ballet music had tended to be mere accompaniment to the dancers onstage. But in his ballets, Tchaikovsky turned the orchestra into an essential ingredient of ballet.

Swan Lake was composed in 1877, partly because Tchaikovsky needed the money. But also, as he wrote, "I have long had the wish to try my hand at this kind of music." The story tells of the doomed Swan Queen who, in Tchaikovsky's version, is saved in the end by the heroic prince. The music is unified by the composer's use of recurring themes, the most famous for the haunting solo oboe with harp, representing the Swan Queen herself.

The Sleeping Beauty came thirteen years after *Swan Lake* and between Symphonies Nos. 5 and 6. The fairy tale of the princess who is put to sleep until the prince awakens her with a kiss is well known, but contains little action. So, Tchaikovsky worked closely with the choreographer, collaborating on every detail, section by section. The result is one of the most colourfully scored ballets, and a brilliant showpiece for the orchestra.

For *The Nutcracker*, the suite, or highlights extracted from the full ballet score, was heard before the premiere of the ballet itself. This time the story came from E.T.A. Hoffmann via a retelling by the elder Alexander Dumas. A little girl receives a toy nutcracker for Christmas and, in her dreams, her toys come to life, and take her on a spectacular journey. Most of the selections in the suite come from Act II and the Land of the Sugarplum Fairy. Here, Tchaikovsky's combination of the exotic with the familiar, and his sense of orchestral colour come to the fore. In the "Dance of the Sugarplum Fairy" he used the newly invented celeste to create a delicate, twinkling sound. And, as in both *Swan Lake* and *The Sleeping Beauty*, he composed a wonderful swirling waltz as the musical highlight – in this case, the "Waltz of the Flowers."

Although Mstislav Rostropovich is known primarily as a great cellist, he is also a talented pianist and conductor. One of his strengths as a conductor has always been the music of his compatriot Tchaikovsky, and he made this recording within a few years of emigrating from the USSR in 1974. Rostropovich's grand sense of the theatre and his warm, outgoing personality come across in spades here. He gets the members of the Berlin Philharmonic to give a warm, red-blooded performance like no other. As the producer of this recording once remarked, "Rostropovich struck sparks off the Berlin Philharmonic!"

■ _____

PETER ILYICH TCHAIKOVSKY: *Ballet Suites*
Berlin Philharmonic Orchestra/Mstislav Rostropovich
DGG The Originals 449 726-2

ANTONÍN DVOŘÁK (1841–1904):
Symphonies Nos. 8 & 9

It was Johannes Brahms who was, at least in part, responsible for the success of the Czech composer Antonín Dvořák. By the 1870s, Brahms had become an influential composer in Vienna. He heard some music by Dvořák, was suitably impressed, and helped arrange government grants for him. Brahms even went so far as to talk to his publisher about taking on the young Czech composer. The publisher Simrock printed some of Dvořák's music and it was received well enough that more was requested. The result was the successful first set of Slavonic Dances, Op. 46, but it was Simrock who made most of the money, not the composer. Nevertheless, it meant that Dvořák's name became recognized internationally, and he never looked back.

Dvořák's music is instilled with the folk music of his country. Like Bedřich Smetana before him and Leoš Janáček after him, Dvořák wanted to fire up a national awareness and pride by using Bohemian or Czech folk material and subjects. His assimilation is gentler than other nationalistic composers, because he wove the ethnic Czech character into an Austro-German musical style.

The Symphony No. 8 was composed in 1889 and premiered in Prague in 1890, with Dvořák conducting. At the time, he was enjoying considerable success, especially in London, and the symphony is one of his sunniest and most optimistic. He wrote to a friend during its composition that his "head was full of ideas." Dvořák wanted to write a work that differed from his earlier symphonies in how his ideas were worked out. And in the Symphony

No. 8, there is a new approach to developing the themes, and in his use of textures as a compositional tool.

In 1892, Dvořák accepted the job of director of the National Conservatory of Music in New York. Interested as he was in folk music, while in the U.S., he absorbed the music of American Indians, the songs of Stephen Foster, and the music of the black population, especially spirituals. At one point, he considered writing an opera based on Longfellow's poem "The Song of Hiawatha." Dvořák believed that there should be no difference between the nationalistic trends in Europe and those in the U.S., and that American music should be based on the culture and folk music of its people.

The Symphony No. 9, subtitled "From the New World," was premiered by the New York Philharmonic Orchestra in 1893. In it, Dvořák showed a marked American influence, especially in the haunting slow movement that has all the attributes of a spiritual. Words were later attached to the main tune and it developed a life of its own as "Goin' Home." But controversy erupted over the idea that an "American" symphony had been composed by a Bohemian. Dvořák downplayed the argument, saying, "I was and remain a Czech composer. I have only shown them the path they might take – how they should work."

Rafael Kubelik was one of the great Czech conductors of the twentieth century. He spent decades outside his native country, in self-imposed exile, returning as a kind of cultural hero in 1990 after the Velvet Revolution and the fall of the communist regime. One of Kubelik's great strengths was the music of Dvořák. He recorded it often, and these accounts from the early 1970s are some of his finest. In them, he was able to catch both the warm Romantic glow of the music as well as its enthusiasm and sensitivity. The Berlin Philharmonic was in top form, and the spacious recorded sound has helped keep these recordings as some of the most coveted in this repertoire.

ANTONÍN DVOŘÁK: *Symphonies Nos. 8 & 9*
Berlin Philharmonic Orchestra/Rafael Kubelik
DGG The Originals 447 412-2

EDVARD GRIEG (1843–1907):
Piano Concerto in A Minor, Op. 16

Norwegian composer Edvard Grieg had studied music in Leipzig as a young man, learning the craft of composition but finding his teachers old-fashioned and rigid. When he returned to Scandinavia, he immersed himself in the region's musical life, composing, conducting, performing as a pianist, and teaching. Grieg soon became interested in establishing a distinct Norwegian musical style and spirit, based on idioms of native folk music and dealing with Norway's legends, heroes, and its dramatic landscape of mountains and fjords. He collected, edited, and published several volumes of Norwegian folk music, and he began to instill his compositions with the flavour of Norwegian folk music, incorporating its style and idiom into his own, rather than quoting it outright. For a couple of years, Grieg composed songs, short piano pieces and chamber music works, making a name for himself in Norway and Scandinavia. Then, in 1869, the premiere of the Piano Concerto in A Minor established him internationally, and he never looked back. From then on, Grieg was recognized as the leading musical figure of Norway, and he was showered with honours and awards, both at home and abroad.

The Piano Concerto was composed in 1868, when Grieg was twenty-five, just a couple of years after his return from studies in Germany. The opening shows the influence of the piano concerto by Robert Schumann, a favourite of Grieg's, but after that Grieg sets out on his own course. He was mainly a composer of songs, and it's the wealth of melodies and rich lyricism of the concerto that has made it one of the all-time favourites, and Grieg's most popular work.

Grieg contrasts the urgency of the first movement, with the rich song-like qualities of the second movement, presented initially by soft, muted strings. The finale is instilled with the energy of a Norwegian folk dance, ending triumphantly with piano, full orchestra, and timpani roll, not unlike the opening. Throughout the concerto the piano is kept in the spotlight with some of the most beautiful and idiomatic writing for the solo instrument ever conceived. It's no wonder that the concerto is a perennial favourite for pianists as well as audiences. A couple of years after the premiere, Grieg visited Franz Liszt, who sight-read the concerto, making comments and suggestions as he went. At the end, he turned to Grieg and said, "Go on, I tell you. You have the stuff!"

Norwegian pianist Leif Ove Andsnes has recorded the Grieg Concerto twice. The first recording helped establish his name in the early 1990s. This is the second one, and it is even finer. Andsnes is able to combine the best elements of the Grieg Concerto into one unified whole. His performance is authoritative, poetic, and captivating, with a freedom that catches the extroverted bravura and virtuosity of the work, without ever losing sight of the more introverted lyricism and tenderness. Mariss Jansons and the Berlin Philharmonic Orchestra provide accurate and sophisticated support, and the clear recording quality brings out the beauty of tone of both pianist and orchestra.

■───

EDVARD GRIEG: *Piano Concerto in A Minor, Op. 16*
Leif Ove Andsnes, Berlin Philharmonic Orchestra/Mariss Jansons
EMI Classics   557 562-2

EDVARD GRIEG (1843–1907):
Excerpts from Peer Gynt

The great Norwegian playwright and poet Henrik Ibsen wrote his drama *Peer Gynt* in 1867. In 1874, he approached Edvard Grieg to write incidental music to go with a planned staging in . Oslo. Grieg was reluctant for a couple of reasons. For one thing, Grieg didn't share Ibsen's keenness for the character of Peer Gynt. He thought that the play was unsuitable for musical adaptation, calling it "the most unmusical of all subjects." Secondly, Grieg probably knew that his talents lay more with the lyrical than with the dramatic. But, eventually, he agreed. The composition of the music occupied him for two years and it was just as tough a struggle as he had originally thought. He pressed on and completed the score in time for the Oslo production in 1876. It was a big success, and many have credited its success more to the strength of Grieg's music than to Ibsen's story.

Peer Gynt is an unusual tale in that it tries to combine epic heroic folklore material with a principal character who is cynical, amoral, and even cruel. The story follows Peer Gynt's life spent searching for love and happiness, and the many adventures he has. At the end, as an old man, he returns home to be with Solveig, his childhood sweetheart, who has always loved him and stayed true to him all these years.

There are many dramatic possibilities and twists of plot in *Peer Gynt*, but Grieg focused more on setting the moods of the scenes rather than describing them. Ibsen felt that the music was too gentle, and lacked the bite of his character and the story. But all the same, the music to *Peer Gynt* has remained a favourite to today.

One of the most famous segments is "In the Hall of the Mountain King," in which Grieg depicts the growing rage of the trolls by repeating a phrase, gradually increasing its dynamics and intensity. "Morning" has been used countless times in radio and television commercials. Grieg described its climax as "the sun breaking though the clouds." One of the darker sections is "Åse's Death," a solemn funereal section that fits with the death of Peer's mother, Åse.

Perhaps because Grieg knew that his music would be more popular than the play it accompanied, he created two concert suites for orchestra alone from the full score. On this recording, Sir Thomas Beecham conducts his own selection from the full score, reinstating the original chorus as well as the soprano, who sings Solveig's part. Beecham had a flair for this kind of music and brought to it a vivid characterization and a sensitive feel for the story's epic nature. Soprano Ilse Hollweg is a warm, faithful Solveig and the Beecham Choral Society and Royal Philharmonic Orchestra are both in top form.

■ _____

EDVARD GRIEG: *Excerpts from Peer Gynt*
Ilse Hollweg, Royal Philharmonic Orchestra, Beecham Choral Society/
    Sir Thomas Beecham
EMI Classics   CDM 566 914-2

NIKOLAI RIMSKY-KORSAKOV (1844–1908): *Scheherazade, Op. 35*

As a boy, Nikolai Rimsky-Korsakov had dreamed of a career in the Russian Imperial Navy. Several of his family members had enjoyed naval careers and some had risen as high as the rank of admiral. By the time he entered the naval academy at the age of twelve, young Nikolai had not only read many books about the sea, but he'd assembled model sailing ships, and could easily quote nautical terms. After graduation, he sailed around much of the world with the Russian Navy for several years. His tour left him with an openness to different peoples, exotic ports of call, and new cultures, and he was strongly influenced by them throughout his life.

His other love was music – a love that eventually won out. In 1861, Rimsky-Korsakov met Mily Balakirev, a musician on a mission to develop a truly Russian style of music, devoid of mainstream European influences. Rimsky-Korsakov joined Balakirev's group of composers that became known as the "Russian Five" or "The Mighty Handful," and consisted of Balakirev, César Cui, Alexander Borodin, Modest Mussorgsky, and Rimsky-Korsakov. Although he had little formal training, Rimsky-Korsakov enjoyed a successful career in music, especially as a teacher at the St. Petersburg Conservatory. He strongly influenced the course of Russian music well into the twentieth century by acting as teacher to Stravinsky, Prokofiev, Glazunov, Liadov, Myaskovsky, and Arensky, among others.

Rimsky-Korsakov's love for exotic cultures and music came together in 1888 for his masterpiece, the great orchestral suite *Scheherazade*, based on *The Arabian Nights*, or *The Thousand and*

One Nights. An evil Sultan, convinced of the faithlessness of woman, puts each of his wives to death after their wedding night. But Scheherazade outsmarts the Sultan by diverting him with fantastic stories of adventure and intrigue, which she spins out over one thousand and one nights. Driven by curiosity, the Sultan postpones her death, each night, to find out how her stories will end. Finally, he gives up on the evil plan and relents altogether.

In *Scheherazade*, two themes are used that recur in all four movements. The first is the gruff, robust theme heard off the top, representing the evil Sultan. That's followed by the tender, sensual solo violin theme that is Scheherazade. The music throughout is almost like a film score – lush, dramatic, colourful, descriptive, and evocative, with many changes of mood and scene. The titles of the four movements provide some of the action, although Rimsky-Korsakov, worried that they would be taken too seriously, later withdrew them. (1) The Sea and Sinbad's Ship, (2) The Tale of the Kalendar Prince, (3) The Young Prince and Princess, (4) The Festival at Baghdad – The Sea – Shipwreck – Conclusion.

The 1990 Telarc recording with Sir Charles Mackerras and the London Symphony Orchestra is one of those rarities where the recorded sound quality and the performance standard are both top-notch. It has often been used by audiophiles as a demonstration disc to impress their friends. On the performance side, Mackerras creates a lush, sumptuous reading that has all the swashbuckling power of an Errol Flynn movie. He's helped by the warm, seductive solo violin of concertmaster Kees Hulsmann. The climactic finale, especially, will give you goosebumps before it ends elegantly and peacefully as Scheherazade finally wins out.

■ ————————————————————————————————

NIKOLAI RIMSKY-KORSAKOV: *Scheherazade, Op. 35*
London Symphony Orchestra/Sir Charles Mackerras
Telarc   CD-80208

GABRIEL FAURÉ (1845–1924): Requiem, Op. 48

In the long lifetime of the French composer Gabriel Fauré, music went through a number of developments and changes. In his youth, the early Romantics Hector Berlioz and Frédéric Chopin were still alive, and by the time of his death in 1924, the transformations wrought by Igor Stravinsky and Arnold Schoenberg had occurred. Yet through it all, Fauré remained consistent to a traditional style, typically French in its clarity and elegance. The American composer Aaron Copland summed him up beautifully when he wrote, "Those aware of musical refinements cannot help admire the transparent texture, the clarity of thought, the well-shaped proportions. Together they constitute a kind of Fauré magic that is difficult to analyze but lovely to hear."

Like other nineteenth-century French composers, Fauré was a church musician for much of his career. Despite the job, he remained a religious skeptic and was never completely comfortable with organized religion. He composed his *Requiem* in the late 1880s, not long after the deaths of both of his parents. But Fauré was never keen to link the work with his parents. When asked why he wrote the *Requiem*, he replied, "For no reason, for pleasure, if I may be permitted to say so."

As Johannes Brahms (another religious skeptic) did in *Ein Deutsches Requiem*, Fauré chose to avoid the terror and threats of damnation that are important elements of other requiems. But where Brahms succeeded by dropping the text of the Mass for the Dead entirely, Fauré achieved his success by using the ancient liturgical text, but downplaying the fear, and emphasizing comfort and solace instead. He once said, "They say that my *Requiem* does not express the terror of death and someone has called it a lullaby of death. But that is how I see death: as a happy deliverance, as a yearning for the joy that lies beyond, rather than as a painful, sorrowful experience."

The Fauré *Requiem* is a soothing work that attempts to console the living, while offering a prayer for eternal rest. It has gentle rhythms and long melodic lines that move step-wise without large leaps, similar to ancient plainchant. The work may be smaller in scope and grandeur than other Requiems, but it is just as powerful in effect and message.

Fauré revised the *Requiem* a number of times and it appeared in several different instrumental makeups. The reasons for his revisions are unclear. It's possible that they made the work more accessible to a broader audience and therefore more saleable. In any case, the differences are not huge. The recommended recording uses the 1893 version, sometimes known as the "church" version, because it calls for a smaller orchestra with no violins or woodwinds. A larger, full orchestra version is better known and is usually the one performed in concert halls.

The earlier 1893 version has greater clarity and its radiant quality is achieved through the voices instead of through the violins and woodwinds. Fauré saved the brass and timpani for the darker, more powerful sections. Conductor Philippe Herreweghe works wonders at balancing his scaled-down vocal and orchestral forces. His account is reverent and restrained, catching the necessary "candlelit" quality of the work.

■ ──

GABRIEL FAURÉ: *Requiem, Op. 48*
La Chapelle Royale, Ensemble Musique Oblique/Philippe Herreweghe
Harmonia Mundi   HMD 941292

SIR EDWARD ELGAR (1857–1934):
Enigma Variations, Op. 36

Sir Edward Elgar was the epitome of the English country gentleman – tall, well-groomed, a bit stodgy and conservative, and usually dressed in tweeds. Even his hobbies of golf, hunting, and kite flying fit the bill. Musically too, Elgar tended to be conservative. Although he lived until 1934, long after many twentieth-century musical styles had been established, Elgar still preferred to look into the rear-view mirror. His music is lush and warm, with its roots in nineteenth-century musical traditions. But in some ways, Elgar's musical imagination and creativity led the way for the English composers who followed him, including Britten, Walton, Vaughan Williams, and Tippett.

Elgar composed the *Enigma Variations* for orchestra between 1898 and 1899. He wrote, "In this music, I have sketched, for their amusement and mine, the idiosyncrasies of fourteen of my friends, not necessarily musicians." On the manuscript score, Elgar marked each variation with initials, a nickname, or asterisks. It wasn't long before the identities of who was being depicted were deciphered – but that's not really the enigma. It doesn't lie in the identification of the people portrayed – it lies in the original theme on which each variation is based.

Elgar never divulged anything about the theme, and compounded the enigma by suggesting that through the entire set of variations another, larger theme is implied but never heard. Over the century since its composition, there have been many attempts to solve the enigma. Everything from "Auld Lang Syne" to a theme from *Parsifal* by Wagner, to the "Prague" Symphony by Mozart, to

"Pop Goes the Weasel" has been suggested! We'll probably never really know, and it doesn't really matter. But music lovers, musicians, and scholars will always enjoy trying to solve the enigma.

English conductor Sir Adrian Boult had known Elgar personally, and the *Enigma Variations* became a popular favourite of his. Boult recorded it no less than four times in his career, the final version (often considered his best), in 1970, when he was a spry eighty-one-year-old. His masterful blend of spontaneity with that English grand manner have never been matched. Each variation is beautifully moulded, but Boult never loses sight of the work as a whole, and lends it a natural flow and progression. It's fresh but authoritative and poised. This is a performance by a great conductor who loved this work, and spent his lifetime conducting it.

■—————————————————————————————

SIR EDWARD ELGAR: *Enigma Variations, Op. 36*
The London Symphony Orchestra/Sir Adrian Boult
EMI Classics   567 749-2

Sir Edward Elgar (1857–1934):
Cello Concerto in E Minor & Sea Pictures

The First World War depressed Sir Edward Elgar terribly. The senseless slaughter of war devastated him, but there was more. It was the end of a way of life for him, both socially and artistically. His life and everything he held dear was changed by the war and swept away forever. He wrote a letter during the war complaining, "Everything good & nice & clean & fresh & sweet is far away – never to return." By 1919, Elgar had almost become a British musical monument. His great works like the *Enigma Variations*, the symphonies, and *The Dream of Gerontius* were behind him. He was held in high esteem, but the new music of Stravinsky, Schoenberg, and others made him worry about becoming obsolete. At the same time, his health, and that of his wife, Alice, was failing. It was in this time of sadness and uncertainty that Elgar composed his Cello Concerto. Although he lived for another fifteen years, this was his last major work. As a result, the Cello Concerto does have a resigned, autumnal mood, but that's not to say it lacks vitality. As he described it, "It's good! Awfully emotional! Too emotional, but I love it!"

One of the problems in writing a concerto for cello is the clarity of the solo instrument. The beauty of the cello lies in its warm mellow tone, which lacks the brilliance of other stringed instruments like the violin, and their ability to cut through a dense orchestral texture. Elgar solved the problem in his orchestration. Although he employed a large orchestra, he rarely used it as a whole. For most of the time the cello is heard, it's accompanied by strings and woodwinds, but not the brass. When Elgar does use the full orchestra, the cello is silent. The orchestra's role is to add colour and support to the soloist.

The Cello Concerto was first performed in London in 1919, but the concert had been poorly rehearsed, the work was not well played and was not well received. The great cellist Pablo Casals then took it up and helped display its true worth.

Elgar's song cycle *Sea Pictures* was composed in 1899, just after the successful premiere of the *Enigma Variations*. Elgar was not a natural in the field of song, unlike his contemporaries Gustav Mahler or Richard Strauss, but in *Sea Pictures* he showed an awareness of text and an ease in composition that foreshadowed his next major work, the oratorio *The Dream of Gerontius*. As in the Cello Concerto, a large orchestra is used, but sparingly, allowing the voice to be prominent. The five songs cover a range of emotions – from nocturnal peace, to a storm at sea, to deep, unflagging love. The second song has a text by Alice Elgar, the composer's wife, but it's the fourth song, "Where Corals Lie," that has become the most popular of the cycle.

The recordings of the Cello Concerto with Jacqueline du Pré and *Sea Pictures* with Dame Janet Baker, both conducted by Sir John Barbirolli, have been best-sellers ever since their original release in the 1960s. They are two of the finest recordings of the music of Elgar – ever. The British cellist Jacqueline du Pré was only twenty when the recording was made. She was destined for a brilliant career, but only a few years later was stricken with multiple sclerosis. She died in 1987. In her short life she became famous for her performances of the Elgar concerto. Like du Pré herself, it's a spontaneous, highly Romantic reading, capturing the sadness and nostalgia of the composer. The slow movement has a passionate, searing intensity.

No one has ever come close to capturing the essence of *Sea Pictures* quite like Dame Janet Baker. The work was viewed as substandard until this 1965 recording turned heads and changed minds. Like du Pré, Baker has a subdued intensity that is riveting.

The warm-hearted Barbirolli was a passionate champion of Elgar, and in these recordings his skill as a sympathetic and supportive musical partner is beyond compare.

■

SIR EDWARD ELGAR: *Cello Concerto in E Minor & Sea Pictures*
Jacqueline du Pré, Janet Baker, London Symphony Orchestra/
  Sir John Barbirolli
EMI Classics   CDC 556 219-2

GIACOMO PUCCINI (1858–1924):
Highlights from La Bohème

It would be unusual for any opera company today to present a season that didn't include one of the three operatic hits by Giacomo Puccini: *La Bohème*, *Madama Butterfly*, and *Tosca*. He is simply that popular. Puccini did compose other works than operas, but they are few and inconsequential.

Puccini came from a long line of musicians from the Tuscany region of Italy. As far back as the early 1700s, Puccinis had occupied respected musical positions in the town of Lucca. Puccini's father had been a music teacher and church musician, and he was expected to follow suit. But, as a teenager, Puccini heard a performance of Verdi's *Aida*, and was electrified. The story goes that he made the decision to become an opera composer that night.

Parts of Puccini's life could have been adapted as opera plots. He had several torrid love affairs, despite being married. Even his marriage was operatically inclined. In his twenties, Puccini had fallen in love with Elvira Gemignani, a married woman with two children in his hometown of Lucca. They moved to Milan and lived together, creating a scandal back in Lucca. Tongues wagged harder when a son was born in 1886. Puccini eventually married Elvira in 1904, after the death of her husband. But the plot thickens. In 1903, Puccini was laid up by an automobile accident. A young local girl was hired to help look after him, and the jealous Elvira suspected an affair between Puccini and the girl. Several years later, Elvira went public with her theory, hurtling accusations and abuse upon the girl. Distraught and embarrassed, the young woman committed suicide. The coroner's report revealed that she had been a virgin, confirming her (and Puccini's) innocence. Her family then sued Elvira, and she was fined and sentenced to five months in jail. But Puccini bought the family off, and the whole matter was dropped. Puccini and Elvira eventually reconciled, but their relationship was never the same.

La Bohème is generally considered to be Puccini's masterpiece, but it was a failure at its premiere in 1896. The opera lacked big scenes, passionate climaxes, and spectacle. Instead, it featured a realistic story about a group of young starving artists in Paris and their loves, joys, and sorrows. The story is partly autobiographical. In his own student days in Milan, Puccini had lived a Bohemian lifestyle, sharing an apartment with several others and hiding from creditors. After a few further productions, *La Bohème* caught on with audiences, and Puccini was well on his way to fame and fortune.

La Bohème is often over-done, in the opera house and on record, with casts and conductors milking every note and word. A direct, no-nonsense approach is usually better, one that allows the work to stand on its own merits, devoid of personal excesses and exaggeration. Sir Colin Davis presents a good, straight version that is direct and refreshing. Katia Ricciarelli and José Carreras as the two young lovers, Mimi and Rodolfo, provide strong singing with good characterization that won't fail to bring out the handkerchiefs. This budget-priced single CD of highlights is good value.

GIACOMO PUCCINI: *Highlights from La Bohème*
Katia Ricciarelli, José Carreras et al.,
Chorus & Orchestra of the Royal Opera House, Covent Garden/
    Sir Colin Davis
Philips Eloquence 468 137-2

Gustav Mahler (1860–1911): Symphony No. 4

Gustav Mahler and Jean Sibelius were two of the great symphonists at the turn of the twentieth century. The two men met in Helsinki in 1907 and reportedly got on quite well together. They discussed a variety of musical topics, including the symphonic form. Sibelius explained to Mahler that he loved the structure and logic of the symphony and how, through them, everything connected. Mahler disagreed. He told Sibelius that the symphony was more than music. It must be like the world – it must embrace everything.

Throughout his life, Mahler wrestled with the reasons for life and death. Where do we come from? Why are we born only to die several decades later? And is the meaning of life finally revealed upon death? These questions obsessed him and his music gives them voice. Every one of his symphonies is on a grand scale, and they include a broad range of human emotion, from joy and happiness to sadness and despair. In the Symphonies Nos. 2, 3, 4, 8, and *Das Lied von der Erde* or *The Song of the Earth*, a song-cycle-cum-symphony, he included human voices and texts. In the others, he used pure orchestral music to deliver his meanings and message.

Mahler composed most of the Symphony No. 4 during the summers of 1899 and 1900, while on holiday from his demanding job as director of the Vienna Opera. It was first performed in Munich in 1901, Mahler conducting. The Fourth is the shortest, sunniest, most relaxed symphony he wrote. The orchestra is of a modest size, for Mahler, and in the finale a solo soprano sings one of the poems from *Das Knaben Wunderhorn* or *The Youth's Magic*

Horn, a collection of medieval German folk poetry which Mahler loved and found inspirational. The soprano describes a child's view of heaven, an innocent and naive idea of a place with good food to eat and games to play. But, as always with Mahler, everything is not quite as it may seem at first, and darkness here lies just beneath the surface. Mahler summed up his Fourth Symphony this way: "In the first three movements, there reigns the serenity of a higher realm, a realm strange to us, oddly frightening, even terrifying. In the finale, the child, which in its previous existence already belonged to this higher realm, tells us what it all means."

George Szell gives a classic and "classical" reading of the Symphony No. 4. It's not hyper-Romantic as some conductors are wont to interpret it. His approach links Mahler to the past and his position in the long line of Austro-German symphonic composers, from Haydn and Mozart to Beethoven, Brahms, and Bruckner. The Cleveland Orchestra in the 1960s, under Szell, was one of the finest in the world, famous for discipline and a warm overall sound, in which each section was clearly delineated. In the finale, the American soprano Judith Raskin nicely matches the orchestra's clarity and purity of sound. This recording is rightly considered one of Szell's finest achievements in Cleveland.

■ —————————————————————————————

GUSTAV MAHLER: *Symphony No. 4*
Judith Raskin, Cleveland Orchestra/George Szell
Sony Classical SBK 46535

CLAUDE DEBUSSY (1862–1918):
Prélude à l'après-midi d'un faune, La Mer, etc.

In many ways, French Impressionism in music was a reaction against German Romanticism. Today, a century later, we can appreciate and enjoy both styles, but at the time, it wouldn't have been easy. Nineteenth-century German Romantic music was typically rich and passionate, thickly textured, and tightly organized by structure and thematic development. French music, in contrast, had always had a certain transparency of line and texture, infused with eloquence and grace. At the end of the nineteenth century, Erik Satie, Claude Debussy, and others wanted to make a break from the music of the German Romantics and create a music that was characteristically French – refined, less complex, lean and economical. Debussy had always been interested in new ideas in music, even in his student days at the Paris Conservatoire, where he often enraged his teachers by refusing to accept time-honoured musical traditions and modus operandi. His desire for new musical concepts and sounds was furthered by his experience hearing Javanese gamelan music at the 1889 Paris Exhibition. Debussy later said, "The age of the aeroplane must have its own music."

With Debussy's early String Quartet and the *Prélude à l'après-midi d'un faune* ("Prelude to the afternoon of a faun"), both composed in the early 1890s, musical Impressionism was born. To many, these pieces mark the beginning of twentieth-century music. The Prelude was inspired by a poem of the same title by the Symbolist poet Stéphane Mallarmé. It's a dreamy description of a half-man/half-goat faun on a hot, hazy summer afternoon, in that wonderful state between being awake and dreaming. The faun sees several nymphs and pursues them. But did he see them or was he dreaming? His feelings grow more intense,-but in the end, he succumbs once again to sleep and returns to his interrupted dream. Debussy never tried to translate the Mallarmé poem literally into music. Instead, through clever but subtle use of the orchestra, he created the hot, hazy midsummer mood, and the half-awake confusion of the faun and his dream.

The *Nocturnes* for orchestra came five years after the Prelude. They are titled "Nuages" (Clouds), "Fêtes" (Festivals), and "Sirènes" (Sirens, as in the mythological sea-nymphs). Again, Debussy worked on orchestral colours, sonorities, and shades, admitting to a friend that the *Nocturnes* were an experiment in "the various combinations that can be made with a single colour, as a painter might make a study in grey."

Debussy was fascinated by the sea, although he spent very little time there except for a couple of seaside holidays. *La Mer*, his three symphonic sketches, was composed in Paris. In it, we get three impressions of the depth, power, and force of the sea. By using a range of effects – incomplete snippets of melody, shifting harmonies, and shimmering colours – Debussy created three unforgettable images of the sea, and the play of sunlight and wind on its surface.

This double-CD set includes all the principal orchestral works by Debussy: *La Mer*, the *Nocturnes*, *Prélude à l'après-midi d'un faune*, *Images*, and more. In his twenty-five year tenure with the Montreal Symphony Orchestra, conductor Charles Dutoit shaped the ensemble into one of the finest French orchestras in the world. With a magical flair for music by Ravel and Debussy, Dutoit combines clear lines and a precise but free approach to rhythm, with shapely phrases, vivid colours, and atmosphere. These are some of the finest recordings of music by Debussy ever done.

CLAUDE DEBUSSY: *Prélude à l'après-midi d'un faune, La Mer, etc.*
Orchestre Symphonique de Montréal/Charles Dutoit
Decca   460 217-2

CLAUDE DEBUSSY (1862–1918):
String Quartet, Op. 10

MAURICE RAVEL (1875–1937):
String Quartet in F

The music of Claude Debussy and Maurice Ravel is often bundled together under the heading of Impressionism, the style developed by the late nineteenth-century French painters such as Monet, Manet, and Renoir. In both art and music, Impressionism was a subtle style in which the feelings and emotions the subject aroused were more important than the subject itself. By using new effects with greater freedom of form and structure, and a variety of colours and sonorities, Debussy sought to create music that left an "impression" on us. The contemporary French literary movement known as Symbolism was similar. In it, writers like Baudelaire, Verlaine, and Mallarmé were more interested in the sounds the words made than their meaning. Today, symbolism is more closely linked to the music of Debussy and Ravel than Impressionism, because it dealt with sounds, rather than images.

Debussy's only string quartet was one of the first examples of musical Impressionism, composed in 1893 when the composer was thirty-one. But in a rare throwback to tradition, Debussy uses a cyclical form, a popular approach of the earlier French composer César Franck, with whom Debussy briefly studied. The Debussy quartet is cyclical and monothematic, meaning that the musical material of the entire piece all stems from the theme stated at the outset. Many other ideas, often used in contrast, do exist, but the opening idea returns in some variation or other, in all four movements. The overall sound and effect of the quartet were so new, it took decades for the work to be fully appreciated. Franck himself apparently described his former pupil's quartet as "nerve-end music."

Ravel's string quartet came ten years later. It is also his only quartet, and it too, gave his teacher some cause for alarm. Ravel studied with Gabriel Fauré, who described the final movement as "stunted, badly balanced, in fact a failure." Ravel had been impressed by the Debussy quartet, and the influence can be heard in the variety of tone colours, as well as the melodic and harmonic effects. Needless to say, Ravel's quartet came under some strong criticism, and he was encouraged to make changes. Debussy wrote to Ravel, "In the name of the gods of music, and in mine, do not touch a single note of what you have written." Ravel took heed of Debussy's advice, but when comparisons between the two quartets became a popular pastime for music lovers in Paris, the relations between the two composers cooled. Whatever friendship that had existed was now dissolved, more because of the warring factions of their respective followers than animosity between the two men. As Ravel wrote to Debussy, "It's probably better for us after all to be on frigid terms for illogical reasons."

The Debussy and Ravel quartets are almost always grouped together, and this recording from 1965 has always been one of the favourites – not only of these two quartets, but of all chamber music recordings. The Quartetto Italiano was a beautifully balanced ensemble, that prided itself in thorough rehearsal and preparation, performing from memory without scores. There used to be many rumours about the members not getting along, not speaking to each other for weeks, despite tours and concerts. But their musical calibre was so high, there was no hint of their strife in their recordings.

■ _____

CLAUDE DEBUSSY & MAURICE RAVEL: *String Quartets*
Quartetto Italiano
Philips   464 699-2

CLAUDE DEBUSSY (1862–1918):
Images & Children's Corner

The piano was Debussy's instrument, but he was never a concert pianist. Still, his piano music is some of the most original ever composed. Under him, the character of piano music, as well as the technique, were changed forever. New colours, subtleties, effects, fingering, pedalling, harmonies, and the use of different scales and modes created a new style of expressiveness for piano music. Debussy wanted to break away from the inherent percussive quality of the piano: he wanted it to sound as if it had no hammers at all. Another example of Debussy's break from tradition was his use of harmony. Before him, chords were linked with what came before and after them in what are known as chord progressions. But Debussy allowed chords to have a life of their own, existing without relationships.

There are two books of *Images*, from 1905 and 1907 respectively, and they contain some of Debussy's most important piano works. (These are not to be confused with the *Images* for orchestra by Debussy.) The first piece of Book I is called "Reflets dans l'eau" or "Reflections in the Water." By using snippets of melody, vague rhythms, and series of chords created by stacking intervals one on top of another, Debussy came up with one of the most evocative water pieces in all music. Many of the harmonies used could be described today as jazz chords, even though they were used here a century ago. In Book II of *Images*, Debussy's explorations of colours and tonal effects continue, almost to the point of the orchestral. The final piece, "Poissons d'Or" or "Goldfish," was apparently inspired by a Japanese lacquer panel that Debussy proudly kept on his writing desk, showing two goldfish swimming beneath an oriental tree. The impression of the play of light on water, and its reflection off the shiny, darting fish under the surface is beautifully captured.

Debussy composed the *Children's Corner* suite a year after *Images*, for his young daughter, Claude-Emma, whom he affectionately called "Chouchou." It's a collection of short pieces, humorous and often satirical in nature, that easily bring to mind characters in books for children. No. 2 is "Jimbo's Lullaby," while No. 3 is "The Serenade for the Doll." The last one and the most famous is "Golliwog's Cakewalk," where Debussy recreates some of the music heard in travelling minstrel shows of the time, and mockingly makes a dig at the opera *Tristan and Isolde* by Wagner.

The piano music by Debussy is often played poorly. Some pianists feel that by creating a dreamy effect, and applying the sustain pedal liberally they are doing it justice. But invariably a clarity of sonorities and textures is what's required to properly bring across Debussy's intent and the subtleties and nuances in the music. Italian pianist Arturo Benedetti Michelangeli was one of the finest in this regard. Although he may have been less successful in other repertoire, in Debussy, Michelangeli was sensuous and elegant, without ever being overindulgent.

■

CLAUDE DEBUSSY: *Images & Children's Corner*
Arturo Benedetti Michelangeli
DGG   415 372-2

RICHARD STRAUSS (1864–1949):
Four Last Songs

Throughout his long life, composer Richard Strauss was in love with the soprano voice. Strauss married a noted soprano, Pauline de Ahna, in 1894, accompanied her in public recitals, and she was the inspiration for many of the prominent and demanding soprano roles in his operas, for example, *Salome, Elektra,* and the Marschallin in *Der Rosenkavalier.* As well as operas, Strauss composed songs throughout his life. The first was at the age of six – a Christmas carol. And the *Four Last Songs,* aptly named, are the capping of a brilliant career in which the female voice played such an important role, as both inspiration and vehicle.

Strauss composed the last of the *Four Last Songs* first – "Im Abendrot" ("At Dusk"), to a poem by Joseph von Eichendorff. It was 1948, he was in his eighties and still reeling from the devastation and destruction of the Second World War, in which he had been linked with the Nazis. The song tells of a couple looking back over their long and happy life together. Weary from their travels and experiences, they turn to the setting sun and ask, "Is this perhaps death?" Strauss was very aware that he was preparing to say farewell. The use of the soprano was an obvious tribute to his wife, Pauline. And in "Im Abendrot," Strauss included an orchestral quote from his earlier tone poem, *Death and Transfiguration.*

Then a new edition of the poems of Hermann Hesse inspired Strauss to compose more songs. The results are "Frühling" ("Spring"), "Beim Schlafengehen" ("Going To Sleep") and "September." As a group, the *Four Last Songs* hint at the passing of time and the resignation to the coming of death. But they are not dark or morose. In the poems selected and the music composed, there's a quiet acceptance – not so much of death itself, but of the end of a fulfilled life. Strauss died in 1949 and the *Four Last Songs* were published and premiered in 1950. They are the glorious last breaths of a great composer.

German soprano Elisabeth Schwarzkopf made part of her successful career singing the songs and the operatic soprano roles of Strauss. She recorded the *Four Last Songs* by Strauss twice – this is the second, and the only one in stereo. Her subtle approach, impeccable diction, and light soprano voice are wonders to hear on their own. But Schwarzkopf also brings the right mixture of reflection and resignation to the songs, making the overall effect very moving. Conductor George Szell and the Berlin Radio Symphony Orchestra are in peak form as well, blending the instruments beautifully with the voice, sympathetic and supportive from beginning to end.

■

RICHARD STRAUSS: *Four Last Songs*
Elisabeth Schwarzkopf, Berlin Radio Symphony Orchestra/
    George Szell
EMI CDM 566 908-2

RICHARD STRAUSS (1864–1949): *Tone Poems*

A tone poem or symphonic poem is a major work for orchestra inspired by a poem, story, person, place, or event. It's programmatic music in that it is narrative or descriptive, as opposed to absolute music, which is free from any extra-musical meaning. The origins of the tone poem reach back as far as Beethoven and his overtures *Egmont* and *Coriolan*. The concert overtures of Berlioz and Mendelssohn continued the trend, but it was Franz Liszt who invented the term and established the form around 1850. One of the pinnacles of tone poem production was reached with Richard Strauss at the end of the nineteenth century.

Don Juan was one of Strauss's earliest tone poems, composed while he was in his mid-twenties. Although the orchestral musicians at the première in 1889 complained of the difficulties of their parts, the audience was impressed and took notice of Strauss's name. The popular womanizer, Don Juan, appears in the folklore of several European countries. One of the best-known portrayals is Mozart's Italian opera, *Don Giovanni*. For his tone poem, Strauss turned to the poem "Don Juan" by Nikolaus Lenau. Here, instead of the lusty successful seducer, Don Juan appears as a man searching for the perfect embodiment of Woman. As a result, Don Juan is the one who suffers here, not the women, and in the end, his search, and his life, are left unfulfilled.

Till Eulenspiegel's Merry Pranks was also based on a folk character. It's believed that Till actually lived sometime in the fourteenth century and that his mischievous pranks and jokes represented the resentment the lower classes felt toward their rulers.

Strauss had originally intended to compose an opera based on the legend, but settled instead on a tone poem, in which Till's escapades are brilliantly and vividly portrayed in music. At the end, according to Strauss, he meets his demise and is sentenced to death. But the composer keeps Till alive by providing an echo of his theme as a ghost of his spirit.

Also sprach Zarathustra (*Thus Spake Zarathustra*) was inspired by the philosophy of Friedrich Nietzsche, although loosely. Strauss wisely didn't try to create a philosophical work, but instead used Nietzsche's theories as a springboard. Strauss wrote, "I meant to convey in music an idea of the evolution of the human race from its origin, through the various phases of development, religious as well as scientific, up to Nietzsche's idea of the Superman. The whole idea of the tone poem is intended as my homage to the genius of Nietzsche."

The opening of *Also sprach Zarathustra* was made famous by its use in director Stanley Kubrick's classic film *2001: A Space Odyssey*. The soft, unresolved ending of the music suggests the uncertainty of Nietzsche's, and others', position.

The Austrian-born conductor Karl Böhm was a good friend of Richard Strauss's as well as a close colleague. Böhm conducted the premieres of two of the operas by Strauss, and one of them, *Daphne*, was dedicated to him. Not surprisingly, Böhm was one of the great Strauss interpreters, and these recordings are testament. He brings a bold, hearty treatment to these tone poems and elicits exquisite playing from the Berlin Philharmonic Orchestra.

■ ───

RICHARD STRAUSS: *Tone Poems*
Berlin Philharmonic Orchestra/Karl Böhm
DGG Eloquence   469 638-2

JEAN SIBELIUS (1865–1957):
Violin Concerto in D Minor, Op. 47

As a boy, Sibelius dreamed of becoming a violin virtuoso, and he devoted himself to mastering the instrument and achieving that goal. But when it hadn't happened by the time he was twenty-five, he wrote, "I had to admit that I had begun my training for the career of an eminent performer too late." But Sibelius's early devotion to the violin was not completely wasted. In 1903, it helped him to create a violin concerto like no other – one that is completely Scandinavian, with a stunning, idiomatic, and original solo part.

The Violin Concerto by Sibelius was first performed in Helsinki in 1904. The premiere did not go well, and the highly self-critical Sibelius withdrew the score and revised it, making it more concise and integrated. The new-and-improved version was heard in Berlin the following year. It was received well by the public, but it took decades before the work became part of the standard repertoire. Most of the reason is due to the difficulty of the solo part. Sibelius calls for the violin soloist to play at fast speeds, often with large, awkward leaps. There are a variety of bow strokes required. Left-hand fingering at quick speeds in the high register of the instrument is tricky, and there's quite a bit of double-stopping called for – playing on two strings simultaneously. But it's not all for show. Gradually, the strength of the music and expression won violinists over, and the Sibelius Violin Concerto took its place in the repertoire, alongside other great violin concertos like the Beethoven, Brahms, and Tchaikovsky.

One of the Concerto's strongest characteristics is its "northern" quality – that beautiful sound that conjures up the bleak landscape of Finland and the country's epic heroic literature. Sibelius once said, "It pleases me greatly to be called an artist of nature, for nature has truly been the book of books for me." The austere opening pages create an eerie and almost hypnotic effect, as the solo violin is first heard amid slowly shifting orchestral strings, like the sun burning through hoarfrost. The second movement is a beautiful, melancholic song for the violin that rises and rises to a passionate and romantic climax. The finale is a rugged, lumbering dance that the English critic and writer Sir Donald Francis Tovey aptly described as "a polonaise for polar bears."

The combination of warmth and lyricism within a bleak, rough-hewn style has sometimes caused the music of Sibelius to be described as "fire and ice." That's what comes immediately to mind when listening to the recording by violinist Cho-Liang Lin, the Philharmonia Orchestra, and conductor Esa-Pekka Salonen. Lin is perfect here, using a clean, silvery tone infused with warmth and tenderness, without too much vibrato. His playing is effortless, and there is a wonderful balance between soloist and orchestra that's nicely caught by the excellent recording.

∎—————————————————————————————————

JEAN SIBELIUS: *Violin Concerto in D Minor, Op. 47*
Cho-Liang Lin, Philharmonia Orchestra/Esa-Pekka Salonen
Sony Classical   SK 44548

Jean Sibelius (1865–1957):
Symphony No. 5 in E-flat, Op. 82

One of Sibelius's most interesting traits is how he presents his musical material. Austro-German composers such as Haydn, Mozart, Beethoven, Schumann, Brahms, and others tended to present their musical ideas clearly up front, even to herald their arrival with introductions. Once stated, the material was then worked on and developed. But Sibelius, and other Scandinavian composers, preferred that their musical ideas emerge from the general din of the orchestral texture – like objects and shapes emerging from a mist.

The Symphony No. 5 by Sibelius was composed in response to the horror of the beginning of the First World War. Sibelius had heard of the assassination in Sarajevo in 1914 that triggered the war, while on a ship in the middle of the Atlantic, travelling back to Finland from the U.S.A. By the time he had settled back into his routine at home, all of Europe was at war. He began work on the Symphony No. 5 for a planned concert in Helsinki to mark his fiftieth birthday. Sibelius was financially strapped at the time, and took on a heavy workload to resolve his money problems. It wasn't in his nature to rush to finish things, but he pushed on valiantly and completed the symphony in time for his fiftieth birthday celebrations on December 8, 1915, when it was first performed in Helsinki, Sibelius conducting. He then revised it several times, which for Sibelius meant making the work more concise and concentrated. It is this concision that is one of the great strengths of this symphony. Sibelius creates a huge, complex structure from the most basic means. Where the Austro-Germans used relationships between keys to drive a symphony, Sibelius used tempo in the first movement of the Fifth, where time seems to shrink as the tempo gets faster and faster. The second movement begins as a delicate theme and variations, but based on a rhythmic idea, not a melody. Then in the finale, Sibelius introduces one of his most famous ideas – a chiming figure for the horns that he claimed came to him after watching a flock of swans fly overhead. This theme has come to be known as the "Swan Theme," although the English writer and critic Sir Donald Francis Tovey referred to it as "Thor swinging his hammer." It emerges out of the rushing, quiet strings, off the top, and is the heart and soul of the movement. Then Sibelius reverses the approach he used in the first movement. He slows everything down gradually, enhancing the arrival of the climax of six isolated, powerful chords that end the symphony dramatically and radiantly.

Sir Colin Davis is one of the contemporary reigning champions of the music of Sibelius, and he's held that honour since he recorded the complete Sibelius symphonies with the Boston Symphony Orchestra in the mid-1970s. Davis's approach to Sibelius is clean and almost impressionistic, rather than lush and highly romantic, and this allows the music to stand on its own better and more objectively. You can't help but be impressed here with the performance quality, as well as the originality of Sibelius, and that's always the stamp of a great recording.

■ ───

JEAN SIBELIUS: *Symphony No. 5 in E-flat, Op. 82*
Boston Symphony Orchestra/Sir Colin Davis
Philips Eloquence   468 198-2

Ralph Vaughan Williams (1872–1958): *Symphony No. 5 and "The Lark Ascending"*

The English composer Ralph Vaughan Williams was a bit of a slow starter. Until he was almost forty, he showed few signs of becoming the master we appreciate today. Well trained in music – he was a student of composers Sir Charles Villiers Stanford and Sir Charles H. Parry at the Royal College of Music in London – he went on to study in Berlin with Max Bruch, and then did a doctorate of music in Cambridge in 1901. After that, Vaughan Williams worked away as a church musician and organist, editing an English hymn book in 1904. Then, something clicked and his life and career changed. He fell under the spell of the English folk song. Just as the Hungarians Béla Bartók and Zoltán Kodály were doing, Vaughan Williams and his friend, the composer Gustav Holst, went out into the countryside to collect native folk music, as performed in the pure, unaltered state.

Vaughan Williams had never been a big fan of the nineteenth-century Austro-German musical tradition, once saying, "To this day, the Beethoven idiom repels me." But in the treasury of English folk song, he found his niche and inspiration. He began to compose music that drew upon the English traditions and idioms he had heard first-hand in the field. The *Norfolk Rhapsody No. 1*, included on the recommended recording, is one such work, and garnered quite a bit of attention when it was first performed. Then in 1908, feeling he lacked a certain refinement and polish, he went to Paris to study with Maurice Ravel. Three years younger than Vaughan Williams, Ravel wasn't quite sure what to do with his new student. After looking over some of his scores, Ravel assigned him the task of writing a minuet in the style of Mozart. Vaughan Williams was taken aback and insulted. He replied, "Now look here, I've come here to learn from you at some expense, and I am *not* going to write a 'little minuet in the style of Mozart!'" Ravel realized his mistake, rescinded the request, and managed to help Vaughan Williams come up with alternatives to the Austro-German musical traditions and styles. From this time on, his music showed more subtleties of atmosphere, colours and effects. He returned to England, composing now with a new confidence, in all forms of music. After the deaths of the English composers Edward Elgar, Gustav Holst, and Frederick Delius, all in 1934, Vaughan Williams found himself billed as the dean of English music. But these kinds of honours and tags never appealed to him, and he later refused both a knighthood and the appointment as Master of the King's Music. Vaughan Williams remained active and continued to compose to the end. He married his second wife at the age of eighty. He died in his sleep in 1958 at the age of eighty-five, the night before overseeing the first recording of his Symphony No. 9.

The Symphony No. 5 is often considered Vaughan Williams's orchestral masterwork. Although no folk songs are actually quoted, few other works by him are so instilled with the flavour and essence of English folk music as the Fifth. It was completed and premiered in 1943 in London, during the Second World War, with the composer conducting. Many at the time thought it would be Vaughan Williams's last testament – his valedictory work. He proved them wrong, living for another fifteen years and producing another four symphonies. The Fifth shows the influence of Ravel, but is dedicated to Sibelius, whom Vaughan Williams admired.

"The Lark Ascending" for violin and orchestra is probably Vaughan Williams's most frequently played work. Composed in 1914, the title comes from a poem by George Meredith. It's a perfect example of Vaughan Williams's skill in depicting nature and landscape in music.

It took years for conductor Bernard Haitink to complete his cycle of the Vaughan Williams symphonies with the London Philharmonic, but the wait was worth it. There's a stolid integrity to his Fifth Symphony and gorgeous playing from all sections of the orchestra. The American violinist Sarah Chang was only fourteen when she recorded "The Lark Ascending," but she was long past being a child prodigy. She brings a youthful energy to the piece, poetic and atmospheric, never lagging in concentration.

■ ──────────────────────────────────────

RALPH VAUGHAN WILLIAMS: *Symphony No. 5*
and "The Lark Ascending"
Sarah Chang, London Philharmonic Orchestra/Bernard Haitink
EMI Classics   CDC 555 487-2

SERGEI RACHMANINOFF (1873–1943):
Piano Concerto No. 2 in C Minor, Op. 18

In a 1923 interview, the great Russian pianist and composer Sergei Rachmaninoff explained, "So much has been written for the piano that is really alien. I believe in what might be called indigenous music for the instrument." The "indigenous" quality of Rachmaninoff's piano music is one of its strengths and beauties. Rachmaninoff wrote idiomatically for his instrument, with big-fisted chords and brilliant cascades of fast notes. His piano music is instilled with a style in which the piano always shines.

His Piano Concerto No. 2 came as an indirect result of the failure of his Symphony No. 1 in 1897. The symphony had been badly rehearsed, performed, and received. But to cap it off, the composer and critic César Cui wrote one of the most scathing reviews in music history: "If there is a conservatory in Hell, and one of its gifted pupils should be given the task of writing a symphony on the Seven Plagues of Egypt, and if he should write a symphony resembling Mr. Rachmaninoff's, his task would have been carried out brilliantly and he would enchant all the inmates of Hell."

Rachmaninoff was devastated and so depressed that he suffered writer's block for several years. In 1900, worried about him, some friends arranged for him to see Dr. Nikolai Dahl, a psychologist well regarded for his use of hypnosis and autosuggestion. Dr. Dahl also happened to be a good amateur musician. Regardless of whether it was because of Dahl's therapeutic treatment of Rachmaninoff, or his ability to conduct confidence-building discussions on a wide range of musical topics, or even the fact that he had an attractive daughter to whom Rachmaninoff was drawn, the composer quickly emerged from his depression and began to compose again. By early 1901 he had finished his Piano Concerto No. 2 and dedicated it to Dr. Dahl. It was first performed later that year in Moscow with Rachmaninoff as the soloist.

The Rachmaninoff Piano Concerto No. 2 is one of the best-loved in the repertoire. The word "romantic" is often overused or misused, but for this work it is entirely fitting. For this reason, some of the concerto's themes have been used by others. They include Noël Coward's film *Brief Encounters*. Pop star Eric Carmen borrowed from the second movement for his 1970s hit "All By Myself." And the big theme from the finale was turned into the Sinatra song "Full Moon and Empty Arms" in 1945.

Pianist Vladimir Ashkenazy was schooled in the great Russian piano tradition and he's made the music of Rachmaninoff a specialty. Ashkenazy and conductor André Previn work as one here, in an account that is clean and direct. There are no gimmicks and no exaggerations, and the technical bravura of the piece is evident but downplayed. By reining in some of the romantic characteristics of the concerto, concentrating instead on sparkle and momentum, both pianist and conductor make the work sound fresh and poetic. It's been a favourite ever since it was released in the early 1970s.

■ ──

SERGEI RACHMANINOFF: *Piano Concerto No. 2 in C Minor, Op. 18*
Vladimir Ashkenazy, London Symphony Orchestra/André Previn
Decca   436 3862

GUSTAV HOLST (1874–1934): *The Planets, Op. 32*

*T*he Planets by Gustav Holst is often used as a demonstration piece by clerks selling stereo systems or speakers. One such clerk once told me that he had been so inundated with *The Planets* over the years, he could barely stand to hear the piece. The broad dynamic range and Holst's brilliant use of orchestral colour may have led the work to become *the* sound system "demo" piece, but it can and should have a life of its own.

Gustav Holst was an English composer, whose continental name stemmed from his German and Swedish ancestry. Holst had very broad interests and tended to immerse himself in them to find inspiration. For example, as a student, Holst had been interested in Hindu literature and philosophy. To be able to set some of the poems to music, he learned the difficult Sanskrit language. It was Holst's interest in the exotic that led a friend to introduce him to astrology in 1913. Holst was fascinated and immediately began to plan a major orchestral work based on the astrological character of each planet. He explained, "These pieces were suggested by the astrological significance of the planets. There is no program music in them, neither have they any connection with the deities of classical mythology bearing the same names. If any guide to the music is required, the subtitle to each piece will be found sufficient, especially if it be used in a broad sense."

The orchestral suite opens with "Mars, the Bringer of War," followed by "Venus, the Bringer of Peace," "Mercury, the Winged Messenger," "Jupiter, the Bringer of Jollity," "Saturn, the Bringer of Old Age," "Uranus, the Magician," and "Neptune, the Mystic." Holst ignored Earth, and at the time Pluto had not yet been discovered.

The Planets is scored for a large orchestra, with organ and a women's chorus. Holst's idiom was modern for its time, and some of the music must have shocked contemporary audiences. But the work was a success from the outset, thanks to Holst's ability to stimulate imaginations about space and the unknown. The entire suite has strongly influenced many subsequent film composers when writing scores to accompany films about alien beings and space travel.

"Mars, the Bringer of War" is one of the most famous movements, violent and belligerent. When it was first heard in 1918, listeners believed it to be a musical picture of the First World War, but Holst had actually composed it before war had broken out in 1914. "Jupiter, the Bringer of Jollity" has become the most popular. It clearly shows another of Holst's interests – the English folk song. The sweeping central tune has even had words added to it, forming the patriotic song, "I Vow to Thee My Country." "Neptune, the Mystic," which closes the work, features the wordless women's chorus. This is pure atmosphere, in the truest sense of the word, as the oscillating women's voices trail off into the depth and void of space.

The Planets is the kind of music that the Montreal Symphony Orchestra and conductor Charles Dutoit did very well. Dutoit's great sense of mood, atmosphere, and orchestral colour served the orchestra very well in French music by Debussy and Ravel. But, as can clearly be heard here, it also came to bear in *The Planets*. "Mars, the Bringer of War" has rarely sounded so brutal, and "Saturn, the Bringer of Old Age" never more atmospheric. This is a 1986 demonstration-quality recording that offers every nuance and detail of this masterful score.

GUSTAV HOLST: *The Planets, Op. 32*
Orchestre Symphonique de Montréal/Charles Dutoit
Decca   417 553-2

ARNOLD SCHOENBERG (1874–1951):
Verklärte Nacht and *Pelléas und Mélisande*

Arnold Schoenberg was almost destined to change the sound and perspectives of music. He was definitely a child of his time. The early years of the twentieth century were fascinating ones, with many new developments in science and the arts that challenged age-old practices. In 1903 the Wright brothers conquered the problem of powered flight. A little earlier, Max Planck had come out with his quantum theory, which turned the world of science and nature on its side. A little later, Albert Einstein announced his theory of relativity, which prompted a re-evaluation of the nature of the entire universe and how it worked. Sigmund Freud was probing the hows and whys of the human mind, and in art, Vassily Kandinsky was painting nonrepresentational works – art that showed no real objects, but depicted merely a collection of shapes and colours.

Schoenberg was born in Vienna, which at the turn of the twentieth century was a hub of fresh ideas and new approaches in both science and art. For hundreds of years, music had been based on keys or tonal centres, around which compositions were based: a symphony in C major, a string quartet in D minor, and so on. Around 1908, Schoenberg began to experiment with atonal music, or music that avoided a strong tonal centre – that sonic polarity that had given music a solid structure for hundreds of years. About fifteen years later, he went even further by creating a twelve-tone method of composition, sometimes known as serialism or dodecaphony. In this method, instead of using a key or tonal centre as the basis of a work, the composer creates a series of notes made up of the twelve tones of the chromatic scale, or all the semitones within an octave. The series of twelve tones was called a tone-row, or series (hence the title serialism), and, as in the age-old musical system, it was subject to certain rules. For example, none of the twelve tones could be repeated until the other eleven had been heard first. So no one note was more important than another – a very democratic system. Once the composer had set the tone-row, he could then invert it, playing it upside down, or in retrograde (backwards), or both (retrograde inversion). These techniques dated back to the days of J.S. Bach and his approach to the form of the fugue. And like Bach, Schoenberg was seeking a way of unifying the structure of music. Schoenberg's students and disciples Alban Berg and Anton Webern also adopted the serial techniques.

Although Schoenberg is viewed today as the father of modern music, he was very well-schooled in the past. He had very little formal training in music, and when asked who his teachers had been he often answered, "Bach and Mozart." Schoenberg had been raised in Vienna when Brahms and Wagner were all the rage. Consequently, he felt that his music was a natural development of the Late Romantic German tradition. He insisted that he was a conservative who had been forced to become a radical, out of need.

Verklärte Nacht and *Pelléas und Mélisande* are both early works by Schoenberg, composed when he was still under the influence of Late Romanticism. But even in these early works, Schoenberg's lack of a strong tonal centre is evident and upset many at the time. These works do illustrate Schoenberg's insistence that his music evolved, instead of being invented.

Verklärte Nacht ("Transfigured Night") is based on a poem by Richard Dehmel. While strolling on a moonlit night, a young woman confesses to her lover that she is pregnant by another man. The lover reassures her that their love is deep enough to overcome the obstacle, and permit the child to belong to both of them.

The symphonic poem *Pelléas und Mélisande* by Schoenberg is based on the same symbolist drama by Maurice Maeterlinck that also inspired the composers Gabriel Fauré, Maurice Ravel, Jean Sibelius, and the opera by Claude Debussy. In the story, two half-brothers vie for the love of the enigmatic Mélisande, resulting in murder.

Conductor Giuseppe Sinopoli leads strong performances of both of the early Schoenberg masterpieces. The reading of *Pelléas und Mélisande* is almost impressionistic in its use of sound and colours. And the *Verklärte Nacht* has a clarity and transparency that give it a romantic refinement, enhancing Schoenberg's link to his musical roots.

■──

ARNOLD SCHOENBERG: *Verklärte Nacht and Pelléas und Mélisande*
Philharmonia Orchestra/Giuseppe Sinopoli
DGG Eloquence 469 690-2

MAURICE RAVEL (1875–1937): *Daphnis et Chloé*

One of the most distinguished performing arts groups of the twentieth century was the Ballets Russes, led by the great impresario Serge Diaghilev. Few businessmen of the arts have had his gift for spotting talent. A partial list of his collaborators would include the composers Maurice Ravel, Claude Debussy, Igor Stravinsky, Manuel de Falla, Sergei Prokofiev, and Erik Satie; the painters Pablo Picasso, Georges Rouault, and Leon Bakst; and the choreographers Michel Fokine, Vaslav Nijinsky, and George Balanchine. Diaghilev's most infamous commission was the ballet *Le Sacre du Printemps* by Igor Stravinsky, which caused a near-riot in Paris at its premiere in 1913. One year earlier, the Ballets Russes had put on the ballet *Daphnis et Chloé*, with music by Ravel, choreography by Fokine, and sets by Bakst. Stravinsky later said of it, "It is not only Ravel's best work, but also one of the most beautiful products of all French music."

The ballet is based on a drama believed to be by the fifth-century Greek poet Longus. It tells the story of the love between Daphnis, the shepherd, and Chloé, the shepherdess. The first two scenes depict their courtship, Chloé's abduction by a band of pirates, and her eventual escape. In the third scene, the two lovers are reunited, Chloé falls into the arms of Daphnis, and all ends joyfully.

Ravel had long had an interest in ancient Greece. He wrote, "My intention was to compose a vast, musical fresco, less concerned with archaism than with faithfulness to the Greece of my dreams, which is similar to that imagined and depicted by French artists at the end of the eighteenth century." In other words, this is not so much a picture of ancient Greece, than an elegant and sophisticated view of ancient Greece.

The work on the ballet progressed slowly, with many arguments between Ravel, Fokine, Bakst, and Diaghilev, each of whom had their own ideas and interpretations. But by June 1912, the differences had been worked out, and the premiere took place in Paris. A year later, the ballet had disappeared from the Ballets Russes repertoire, causing a rift between Ravel and Diaghilev. But Ravel wisely made two concert suites from the ballet, and the music survived largely due to concert performances of these. Although this is how the music is often heard today, especially the Suite No. 2, it's the full ballet score that has the most impact.

Ravel's score clearly shows his genius for orchestral colour and atmosphere. He was one of the greatest of orchestrators, and nowhere is this better exhibited than in *Daphnis et Chloé*.

This 1980 recording was one of the first digital recordings and one of the first made with Charles Dutoit and the Orchestre Symphonique de Montréal. Dutoit and the OSM went on to record some eighty recordings together, much of it French orchestral repertoire, for which they became world-famous. Dutoit's great talent is his ear for orchestral colour and textural clarity. The sound of the orchestra here is seductive and ravishing, flexible, refined, and spontaneous. It's a recording of Ravel's masterpiece that will be hard to top.

■ ───────────────────────────────

MAURICE RAVEL: *Daphnis et Chloé*
Orchestre Symphonique de Montréal/Charles Dutoit
Decca 458 6052

MAURICE RAVEL (1875–1937):
Gaspard de la Nuit

Although the complete music for solo piano by Maurice Ravel is not large, it is some of the most important we have. By combining French clarity and elegance with the virtuosity of Chopin and Liszt, Ravel came up with many new piano effects and techniques of expression. Even his older French colleague Claude Debussy was influenced by Ravel's writing for the instrument. But where Debussy's piano music evokes the impressions an object creates in listeners, Ravel's is more direct, going as far as describing the object itself. The great French-born pianist Walter Gieseking described Ravel's piano music as, "the most pianistic ever written, making the most perfect and universal use of the resources of the modern piano."

Gaspard de la Nuit was composed by Ravel in 1908, based on nineteenth-century poetry by Aloysius Bertrand. Ravel had been introduced to the Bertrand poems as a student and had read them repeatedly. Subtitled "Three Poems for Piano," the three parts of the triptych are "Ondine," "Le Gibet," and "Scarbo." They are haunting, macabre, and even grotesque images that bring to mind mysterious lakes, castles, tolling bells, and nocturnal apparitions.

"Ondine" tells the story of the fairy-tale water nymph's attempt to seduce a mortal into joining her in her underwater palace. When he tells her he is in love with a mortal, Ondine laughs and departs in a spray of water. The images of glistening, shimmering water have rarely been better caught, in music or painting.

"Le Gibet," "The Gallows," paints the Bertrand poem of "a bell which tolls from the walls of a city beyond the horizon, and the corpse of a hanged man reddened by the setting sun." The soft but relentless B-flats played throughout provide an eerie chill to the piece, capturing the macabre character of the poem, and reminding one of the subtle degrees of terror and tension found in the poetry of Edgar Allan Poe. This quality for which Ravel was obviously striving can be seen in his instruction to the performer: "sans expression." "Le Gibet" is a masterpiece of musical suspense.

The final poem is "Scarbo," the demonic gnome who brings us nightmares as we sleep. This is one of the most difficult of all piano pieces ever written. It was once said that to play it, the pianist must have wrists of steel and eyes in his fingers. The quick, nervous motions of the gnome are brought to mind by the fast, repeated figures and rhythms, heightened by long pauses. At the end, Scarbo disappears without a trace.

The qualities needed by a pianist to successfully bring across *Gaspard de la Nuit* are all held in spades by the Yugoslavian-born, Moscow-trained Ivo Pogorelich. A brilliant technique, spontaneity, variations of tone colour and shades, clarity, sensitivity and originality are Pogorelich's hallmarks. They all come together here for a magical, spine-tingling interpretation of Ravel's piano masterpiece. Pogorelich's reading of *Gaspard* is one of the finest ever made, with no competitors in sight.

■────────────────────────────────────

MAURICE RAVEL: *Gaspard de la Nuit*
Ivo Pogorelich
DGG 463 6782

MAURICE RAVEL (1875–1937):
Piano Concertos

Maurice Ravel composed his two piano concertos at the same time, and they were premiered within a year of each other in the early 1930s. Working on two concertos simultaneously was a stimulating experience for the composer. Consequently, the two works share a number of similarities, but by no means are they completely alike. Ravel wrote, "The music of a concerto should, in my opinion, be light-hearted and brilliant, and not aim at profundity or at dramatic effects. It has been said of certain great classics that their concertos were written not 'for,' but 'against' the piano. I heartily agree."

In 1929, Ravel was approached by pianist Paul Wittgenstein to compose a piano concerto with a solo part for the left hand alone. Wittgenstein had lost his right arm in the First World War, but determined to continue a performing career, he commissioned several composers to write works for the left hand, including Sergei Prokofiev, Benjamin Britten, Paul Hindemith, Erich Wolfgang Korngold, and Richard Strauss. Intrigued by the challenge of the commission, Ravel studied left-handed piano works by earlier composers, and sat down to write. The Concerto for the Left Hand was completed in nine months. In the late 1920s, Ravel had toured the United States and had enjoyed the jazz that he had heard, incorporating it into some of his own music on his return. Of his concerto, he wrote, "In a work of this kind, it is essential to give the impression of a texture no thinner than that of a part written for both hands." This aspect is one of the reasons for the success of the concerto. Ravel's keen ear and sense of orchestration come to bear when the solo piano and orchestra are playing together. The texture is always transparent, allowing the piano part to shine through.

The Piano Concerto in G by Ravel also contains the influence of jazz, and Ravel worked longer on it than for the Concerto for the Left Hand. It's curious that the scoring for this piano concerto, for both hands, has a thinner texture than that of the concerto for the left hand. Of this one he wrote, "[It] is a concerto in the truest sense of the word: I mean that it is written very much in the same spirit as those of Mozart and Saint-Saëns." Mozart and Saint-Saëns may have provided the spiritual impetus, but the concerto also shows influences of George Gershwin, Igor Stravinsky, and the music of Ravel's native Basque region, which straddles the Spanish border with France. The two piano concertos were the last major works Ravel was to compose. He died after a long illness in 1937.

Pianist Krystian Zimerman and conductor Pierre Boulez were born to make music together. Both approach this music by Ravel with clarity and elegance, always aware of the importance of texture laid out by the composer. But wit and fun are also important ingredients. Pianist and orchestra work as one in a performance that is as clear and sharp as cut crystal.

■ ────────────────────────────────────

MAURICE RAVEL: *Piano Concertos*
Krystian Zimerman, Cleveland Orchestra &
   London Symphony Orchestra/
Pierre Boulez
DGG   449 213-2

MANUEL DE FALLA (1876–1946):
Nights in the Gardens of Spain & The Three-Cornered Hat

The existence and popularity of twentieth-century Spanish classical music is mostly due to a single man: Felipe Pedrell (1841–1922).
He struggled for success as a composer throughout his life, making
ends meet as a teacher, musicologist, music critic, and editor. Pedrell
had his greatest success as a teacher and strongly influenced a generation of Spanish composers, including his students Isaac Albeniz,
Enrique Granados, and Manuel de Falla. Pedrell realized that the
hope and future of Spanish music were rooted in its history and
folklore. He encouraged his students to turn their attention to the
music and culture of Spain for inspiration as well as material.

Manuel de Falla was on the path to becoming a virtuoso
concert pianist until he became a student of Pedrell's. Recognizing
his talent, Pedrell steered Falla toward composition. Falla changed
course and dedicated himself to the composition and cause of
Spanish music, which reached its golden age in the works of Falla,
Isaac Albeniz, Enrique Granados and later, Joaquin Rodrigo.

In 1917, Falla staged a pantomime based on the old Spanish
folk tale of the Corregidor and the Miller's Wife. The great dance
impresario Serge Diaghilev of the Ballets Russes attended one
performance and immediately saw its potential. He urged Falla
to transform his pantomime into a full-fledged ballet score, and
Falla set to work with the choreographer Leonide Massine
and set and costume designer Pablo Picasso. The ballet was titled
The Three-Cornered Hat, after the huge hat worn as a badge of
office by the *corregidor*, or governor. It was successfully premiered
in London in 1919.

The story is launched by the arrest of the miller, which enables the *corregidor* to flirt with the miller's captivating wife. She teases and encourages the *corregidor*, until, during a chase, he tumbles over a bridge and into the mill stream. The miller's wife fishes him out, and the *corregidor*'s wet clothes are hung out to dry. The miller comes home, discovers the wet clothes, and assumes the worst. He then puts on the *corregidor*'s clothes and sets out to try his luck with the *corregidor*'s wife. The finale is a scene of mistaken identity and confusion, but everything ends happily, with the miller and his wife reunited, and all is forgiven.

In non-theatrical music, Falla's greatest success was the concerto-like work for piano and orchestra called *Nights in the Gardens of Spain*, completed in 1915. In it, Falla depicted three Spanish gardens. The first is the Generalife, the fragrant garden surrounding the summer palace of the Moorish kings in Granada known as the Alhambra. (*Generalife* comes from the Arabic *jennat al arif*, or the builder's garden.) The second impression is an unidentified garden off in the distance. And the third is set in the gardens of the Sierra de Cordoba – a festival of gypsy singing and dancing, ending in a mood of peace and mystery.

Daniel Barenboim conducts a vibrant and vivid version of *The Three-Cornered Hat*, ably joined by mezzo-soprano Jennifer Larmore. The Chicago Symphony Orchestra is in top form, responding beautifully to Barenboim's colourful and sensuous interpretation and revelling in the dashing rhythms. In *Nights in the Gardens of Spain*, Barenboim moves over to the piano keyboard, leaving the conducting duties to the great Spanish tenor Placido Domingo. Barenboim and Domingo work at the colours and textures, to the point where you can almost imagine the perfumes of the fragrant gardens. The piano is never too much forward, instead it's correctly balanced with the orchestra in a subtle, impressionistic, and transparent recording.

■ ———————————————————————————————

MANUEL DE FALLA: *Nights in the Gardens of Spain &*
   The Three-Cornered Hat
Jennifer Larmore, Placido Domingo, Daniel Barenboim
Chicago Symphony Orchestra
Teldec 0630-17145-2

Spanish Guitar Music

The guitar is one of the most popular instruments of all time, and its links to Spain and Spanish music have always been close. Many of the great guitar virtuosos in history have been Spanish, and there's a great deal of Spanish music composed for the piano, or for orchestra, that attempts to simulate the sound and style of the guitar. But the origins of the guitar in Europe are cloudy. There are some who believe that the instrument goes back as far as ancient Greece and the *kithara*. Others feel that the guitar may have been introduced to Europe by the Arabs around the Middle Ages. Still others insist it is of oriental origins. Whatever its history, in Europe the guitar developed as part of the lute family of instruments. In essence, a guitar is a short-necked lute with a flat body.

Early guitars were smaller, with only four or five strings, instead of the six or more of today's guitars. The left hand worked the fingerboard. The little finger of the right hand rested on the instrument, while the thumb and first two fingers plucked the strings. The music played was notated in tablature, a system that uses letters, numbers, or other signs instead of the standard musical staff notation of clefs, lines, spaces, and notes. In tablature, the player is told how to produce the pitch required – where to put his fingers on the fingerboard, rather than what pitches to play. By the time of the Baroque, staff notation replaced tablature and the sixth string was added to the instrument. Like most art and music of that period, Baroque guitars were highly decorated. The strumming of the strings and other techniques were developed, and an alphabetical system of notating the left-hand chords began.

The guitar became quite popular at the European courts, especially as an accompanying instrument in songs. Then, with the technological advances of the Industrial Revolution in the nineteenth century, the modern guitar was born. The wooden tuning pegs were replaced by more accurate machine heads, the frets became fixed and made of ivory, ebony, or metal, and the flat back became standard.

The early nineteenth-century guitarist-composers Fernando Sor and Mauro Giuliani did much to help establish a repertoire of large-scale works, with concertos and chamber music. But, by the twentieth century, the guitar still lacked the suitable concert repertoire enjoyed by other concert instruments, like the piano or violin. It was the great Spanish guitarist Andres Segovia who brought the guitar into the concert limelight, making many transcriptions of existing music and asking composers to write for him and his instrument.

The recommended recording features a huge variety of Spanish music for the solo guitar, either originally composed for the instrument or in transcription, from the sixteenth to the twentieth centuries. Included are works by Sor, Gaspar Sanz, Tarrega, Albeniz, Granados, de Falla, and Rodrigo. The Spaniard Narciso Yepes was a talented guitarist, lutenist, and composer. Like Segovia before him, Yepes did much to help establish and expand the repertoire for his instrument by searching out and publishing thousands of old scores. A specialist in Spanish and baroque music, he created the ten-string guitar in 1964 and played it almost exclusively until his death in 1997.

■

MALAGUEÑA: *Spanish Guitar Music*
Narciso Yepes
DGG Eloquence   469 649-2

OTTORINO RESPIGHI (1879–1936):
Pines of Rome, Fountains of Rome

Italians invented opera at the beginning of the Baroque era, around the turn of the seventeenth century. While, later on, they excelled in instrumental music, for the most part, after the Baroque, for about two hundred years, Italian composers focused on opera at the expense of orchestral and instrumental music. Rossini, Bellini, Donizetti, Verdi, and Puccini are known primarily for their advances and successes in opera; instrumental and orchestral music plays a minor role in their output. But at the beginning of the twentieth century, some of the younger Italian composers hoped to return to the golden age of Italian instrumental music and long-lost traditions. Ottorino Respighi was at the forefront of this movement.

Respighi came from a family of musicians. His grandfather had been a violinist and organist, his father a pianist and music teacher. After studies in his hometown of Bologna, Respighi sought travel, experience and further study, and landed a job in St. Petersburg as a violist in the Russian Imperial Opera orchestra. For two seasons, while he gained experience in the pit, he studied composition with Nikolai Rimsky-Korsakov, one of the great Russian teachers and a noted master of orchestration. On his return to Italy, Respighi made his living as a solo violinist, and as a violist in a piano quintet, composing all the while. In 1913, he was appointed a professor of composition at the Santa Cecilia Academy in Rome. And in 1917, he had his first major success as a composer with the symphonic poem *Fontane di Roma* ("Fountains of Rome"). The work was an instant success, championed by none other than Arturo Toscanini, which only added to its acclaim. *Fountains of Rome* doesn't so much present musical pictures of fountains, as much as it creates mood and atmosphere. Four Roman fountains are captured at different times of the day: dawn, mid-morning, noon, and sunset.

Eight years later, Respighi outdid himself with another fantastic symphonic poem, *Pines of Rome*. It became his most popular composition. Once again, he presented four musical pastiches played without a break, captured at four different times of day. But this time, rather than creating mood and atmosphere, *Pines of Rome* deals with nostalgic thoughts of Roman history and landscape. It is on an even grander scale than *Fountains*, with even more brilliant orchestral effects. The final section, "Pines of the Appian Way," begins softly in dawn mists, then builds slowly into a triumphant march, a vision of past military glories along the famous Roman road. It is one of the greatest crescendos in the entire orchestral literature, and few listeners can avoid being moved by its clamorous conclusion. Respighi rounded out what's come to be known as his "Roman trilogy" with *Feste Romane* ("Roman Festivals") in 1928.

These brilliant and colourful Respighi scores were the kind of pieces that the Montreal Symphony Orchestra excelled at playing under former music director Charles Dutoit. *Pines of Rome* became a kind of party piece for Dutoit, not only in Montreal, but in his guest conducting around the globe. Dutoit tried to get beyond the sheer brilliance of Respighi's scores and work away at the expressive possibilities. They're not as obvious, but well worth it in the long run. Dutoit's great sense of colour and atmosphere, witnessed in his recordings of music by the French Impressionists and Stravinsky, worked very well for him here, in Respighi, as well.

■ ──

OTTORINO RESPIGHI: *Pines of Rome, Fountains of Rome*
Orchestre Symphonique de Montréal/Charles Dutoit
Decca 476 1514

BÉLA BARTÓK (1881–1945):
Concerto for Orchestra

Hungarian composer Béla Bartók once told an interviewer that he had been born twice. The first time was in 1881. The second time was about 1905, when a maid cleaning Bartók's apartment, sang as she went. The unusual shape of the melody, and its exotic turns, caught Bartók's keen ear. The maid was unable to tell Bartók where the tune came from or who wrote it. All she knew was that her mother and grandmother had sung it to her as a child.

Between 1905 and 1918 Bartók went out into the countryside and collected, recorded, and edited thousands of central European folk songs and dances. He saw to it that they were published, and they form an invaluable collection of ethno-musicological research. If it hadn't been for Bartók and his friend, fellow composer and compatriot Zoltán Kodály, most of this material would have been lost.

Bartók also incorporated his knowledge and love of Hungarian, Slovakian, Rumanian, and Transylvanian folk music into his own. The influence is not so much direct as it is idiomatic. It can be heard in his choice of scales or modes, as well as in the textures and rhythms.

The public was slow to come to the music of Bartók. Ears that had been weaned on Strauss waltzes and Brahms symphonies found the angular, awkward tunes and jarring rhythms of Bartók strange.

By 1943, Bartók had fled wartorn Europe, settling in the United States. Almost destitute and dying from leukemia, he was visited in his New York hospital room by Serge Koussevitzky, the conductor of the Boston Symphony Orchestra. Unknown to

Bartók, two of his Hungarian fellow musicians, violinist Joseph Szigeti, and conductor Fritz Reiner, had put Koussevitzky up to commissioning a work from Bartók to help his dire financial situation. Szigeti and Reiner were both aware of Bartók's pride, and they knew that if he even suspected a commission was being offered to him out of charity or pity, he would refuse it. Koussevitzky, who had been properly briefed by Szigeti and Reiner, told Bartók that his foundation insisted on paying half of the fee up front, and the other half on completion of the work, and pressed a cheque into Bartók's hand. Bartók was flattered, but worried that he wouldn't live long enough to finish the work. The wily Koussevitzky persisted though, and by the time he had left the hospital room, he had Bartók's agreement.

Most of the work was composed at Saranac Lake in upstate New York in the summer of 1943. The first performances took place in Boston in December 1944 and Bartók was there to hear the audience's enthusiastic response. It was his last completed work. He died in New York nine months later.

The title "Concerto for Orchestra" comes from Bartók's treatment of the orchestra. He wrote, "The title of this symphony-like orchestral work is explained by its tendency to treat single instruments or instrumental groups in a 'concertante' or soloistic manner." At one point or another, every principal orchestral musician is asked to play solo. Yet it's the overall effect of the ensemble, not the virtuosity of the individuals, that forms the impact.

For decades, the benchmark recording of the Concerto for Orchestra featured the Chicago Symphony Orchestra conducted by Fritz Reiner, one of the men responsible for the commission, who knew Bartók personally. But in 1997, the Budapest Festival Orchestra and conductor Ivan Fischer recorded it for Philips, and this has now become my favourite. Fischer and his Hungarian musicians exude a love for and knowledge of this music like no others. They play their hearts out in work that teems with life, despite being written by a composer on his deathbed. Clarity, articulation, and energy are excellent, but there's also a keen awareness of the mystery and importance of this twentieth-century masterpiece.

■

BÉLA BARTÓK: *Concerto for Orchestra*
Budapest Festival Orchestra/Ivan Fischer
Philips   456 575-2

BÉLA BARTÓK (1881–1945):
String Quartets

The string quartets by Béla Bartók are six of the greatest chamber music works in the repertoire, ranked equally as high as those by Beethoven from a century earlier. They trace the journey of Bartók's development as a composer, clearly showing the evolution of his original style.

Bartók composed the six quartets over a period of thirty years, from 1908 to 1939. Quartets Nos. 1 and 2 show the influence of late Romanticism and Impressionism, and the impact of Bartók's extensive research and collection of central European folk music and dance. In the third and fourth quartets, there's a move away from conventional tonality and expression, with structural concision and concentration. And in the last two quartets, Nos. 5 and 6, there's a return to tonality with a more traditional musical language. The Quartet No. 6 was the last major work by Bartók before he fled Europe at the outbreak of the Second World War and settled in the United States. In 1945, the year of his death, he began to sketch the opening of a seventh quartet, but left it incomplete.

Bartók had been trained as a pianist, not a string player, and it's possible that this led him to experiment more freely with new sonorities and modes of expression in string quartet composition. As well as exhibiting many musical styles and idioms, the Bartók quartets also show many new performing techniques. There are eerie glissandos, or the quiet sliding up or down the fingerboard of the instruments, which produces a glassy effect, and many off-beat accents suggest the link to folk music. Sometimes Bartók calls for the players to strum their string instruments like guitars instead of using the bow. He also uses mutes and instructs the musicians to play *sul ponticello*, or on the bridge of the instrument to create haunting effects. Several passages call for double and multiple stopping – the playing of more than one string at a time. And there's the string technique that's come to be known as "the Bartók pizzicato." This is an original and highly effective sound that's created by plucking the strings so hard that they snap back and hit the fingerboard.

No other field of musical composition inspired Bartók as much as the string quartet. And the six he wrote clearly show him to be an original musical thinker, and a very expressive composer of great skill and craft.

Many quartets approach the Bartók quartets with a rustic, rough-hewn sound, stressing the folk music qualities. But the Hagen Quartet, following Bartók's instructions to the letter, fashion a much more sophisticated sound – lean, clean, and pure with a huge range of colours and powerful effects. As a result, these recordings are insightful and ear-opening. They have power and energy as well as warmth, delicacy, and intimacy.

■ ───────── ──────────────────

BÉLA BARTÓK: *String Quartets*
The Hagen Quartet
DGG 463 576-2

IGOR STRAVINSKY (1882–1971):
The Firebird, Petrushka, and Le Sacre du Printemps

In the world of twentieth-century dance, the name Serge Diaghilev stands out. He was the great Russian impresario and founder of the Paris-based company, the Ballets Russes. He was a shrewd businessman and an innovative artistic administrator, with an eye for talent. Diaghilev commissioned ballet scores from such composers as Maurice Ravel, Erik Satie, Manuel de Falla, Claude Debussy, Sergei Prokofiev, and also Igor Stravinsky. He employed the talents of Pablo Picasso and Leon Bakst as set and costume designers. And the choreographers Leonide Massine, Michel Fokine, and George Balanchine all worked for him.

In 1909, Diaghilev got the idea for a ballet based on the old Russian tale, "The Firebird." He approached Anatol Liadov to compose the score, but Liadov dawdled with it, and missed his deadline. In the meantime Diaghilev heard some music by Igor Stravinsky, a twenty-seven-year-old student of Rimsky-Korsakov's, and was impressed. Taking a huge gamble, Diaghilev turned to Stravinsky for the ballet, and the result was *The Firebird*, a magical folk story of good versus evil, complete with a supernatural ogre, beautiful princesses, and a happy ending. It was premiered in Paris in June 1910 and rocketed Stravinsky to stardom. From then on until his death in 1971, he was viewed as one of the great modern composers and the leader of the avantgarde in music. Stravinsky later compiled several suites of music from *The Firebird* for concert use, but the most powerful experience comes from hearing the full ballet.

Always the good businessman, Diaghilev realized he was on to a hot property and was keen to repeat the success of *The Firebird*. Stravinsky had been working on a piece for piano and orchestra that outlined the life of a puppet. After hearing some of the music, Diaghilev, realizing its balletic potential, encouraged Stravinsky to turn the work into another full-length ballet. The result was *Petrushka*, the Russian version of the universal puppet character of Punch, Pierrot, or Harlequin. Set amid the bustling crowds at a Shrovetide fair, the story hovers around an unlikely puppet ménage à trois. Petrushka longs for the beautiful Ballerina but she's more interested in the Blackamoor. A fight ensues, and the jealous Petrushka is killed by the Blackamoor. But in the end, Petrushka's ghost appears on the puppet booth roof, mocking all that has taken place. Petrushka was first performed in Paris in 1911, within a year of the success of *The Firebird*.

Less than two years later, Stravinsky wrote yet another ballet for Diaghilev. This time it was the story of ancient pagan rites and rituals at springtime, called *Le Sacre du Printemps* or *The Rite of Spring*. The premiere in Paris in 1913 led to a riot in the theatre, caused just as much by the crude, deliberately awkward movements of the half-naked dancers, as by Stravinsky's score. Pushing melody to the background and bringing rhythm to the fore, Stravinsky created music that caught the primitive nature of the pagan tribes in the story. Never before had an orchestral work broken the rules of melody, harmony, and rhythm quite like this. *Le Sacre* grabs us in a primal way – through our basic reaction to rhythm. Even today, many find *Le Sacre* disturbing and crude. But it is recognized as one of the masterpieces of ballet, and of all music.

These recordings of the three major ballets by Stravinsky with Sir Colin Davis conducting the Concertgebouw Orchestra of Amsterdam were made in the 1970s. In *The Firebird*, Davis creates a magical, colourful world that slowly opens up, enhancing the mystery of the story. The slower sections are atmospheric, and the faster ones energetic and exciting. In *Petrushka*, the standard of performance of the Concertgebouw Orchestra really shines. It's precise and concise, with great clarity of textures and line. Recordings of *Le Sacre du Printemps* can often sound cacophonous and uncontrolled, but Davis brings out the music of the score, concentrating on structure, sonorities, clarity, and texture instead of just energy and momentum. All three ballets are in their complete versions.

■ ──

IGOR STRAVINSKY: *The Firebird, Petrushka, and Le Sacre du Printemps*
Concertgebouw Orchestra of Amsterdam/Sir Colin Davis
Philips   464 744-2

IGOR STRAVINSKY (1882–1971):
The Symphony of Psalms

In 1929, the Russian-born conductor of the Boston Symphony
Orchestra, Serge Koussevitzky, asked four composers to write
major works honouring the orchestra's fiftieth anniversary in
1930. The composers were Sergei Prokofiev, Arthur Honegger,
Albert Roussel, and Igor Stravinsky. Stravinsky happily accepted
the invitation and, at first, thought about writing a symphony
for the occasion. But traditional symphonic form never appealed
much to him, and he began to drift toward a work for choir and
orchestra, in which both would be equally important. A little
earlier, Stravinsky had returned to his Russian Orthodox roots,
after years away, discovering solace, as well as creative inspiration.
The Symphony of Psalms was the result, one of the masterpieces of
the twentieth century. Stravinsky wrote of it, "It is not a symphony
in which I have included psalms to be sung. On the contrary, it is
the singing of the psalms that I am symphonizing."

The work is scored for mixed choir and a large orchestra,
including two pianos but without clarinets, violins, or violas.
These omissions create an orchestral sound that is dark and bur-
nished, as Stravinsky wanted to create music that kept feeling
and sentimentality out of the mix. He once wrote, "Rhythm and
motion, not the element of feeling, are the foundation of musical
art." He also used the more impassive Latin versions of the psalms,
rather than a modern translation. The choir is used without solo
voices, making a universal, rather than personal statement. And
Stravinsky used *ostinatos*, or the repetition of musical patterns, as
well as a double fugue, to underscore the symphony's intellectual

elements and downplay emotion. Like other works by Stravinsky, *The Symphony of Psalms* is a wonderful balance between intellect and unadorned emotion. It is highly expressive, but without sentimentality.

The three movements express three of the essentials of worship: prayer, thanksgiving, and praise. The first movement, with parts of Psalm 39 of the King James version of the Bible, resembles ancient chant, another earlier form of non-sentimental music. The second movement, from Psalm 40, includes the double fugue – one for the instruments and one for the voices, cleverly combined at the end to signify gratitude. The finale is Psalm 150, a wonderful hymn of praise, unusual in its setting of the text. The opening Alleluia is a slow, reserved statement, instead of the more usual joyous proclamation. The following Laudate Dominum (Praise God) is distant and restrained. The music then builds to a climax, but returns to slow and quiet at the end. In avoiding sentiment, Stravinsky makes us hear the words anew, gaining a fresh understanding of their meaning.

Conductor Pierre Boulez is also a talented composer and always brings a composer's ear for detail to his recordings. Clarity and transparency are always front and centre for him, and the result here is a reading of crisp rhythms and direct intensity. In his younger days, Boulez was an outspoken critic of Stravinsky, but he subsequently changed his view and for decades has been one of the great Stravinsky champions, and one of the greatest exponents ever recorded. Also included in this recording are Stravinsky's Symphonies of Wind Instruments and the Symphony in Three Movements.

■ ───

IGOR STRAVINSKY: *The Symphony of Psalms*
Berlin Radio Choir, Berlin Philharmonic Orchestra/Pierre Boulez
DGG 457 616-2

ALBAN BERG (1885–1935) AND ANTON WEBERN (1883–1945):
Music for String Quartet

Alban Berg and Anton Webern were the two most successful students of Arnold Schoenberg and the three men are sometimes known as the "Second Viennese School," as opposed to the "First Viennese School" – Haydn, Mozart, Beethoven, and Schubert. In some ways, both Berg and Webern surpassed their teacher in their new approaches to music. But, like Schoenberg, they were both products of nineteenth-century German Romanticism, and developed their ideas out of their love and knowledge of the music of Brahms, Wagner, Mahler, and Richard Strauss.

Like his teacher, Berg had little formal musical training. He dabbled in the writing of songs as a teenager, but his musical career did not begin in earnest until he started to study with Schoenberg in 1904. Schoenberg, Berg, and Webern began to compose music that worked away from tonality, or music that was based around a tonal polarity or centre. Berg's Lyric Suite for string quartet was his first foray into Schoenberg's serial method of composition, where the raw material of the music is presented as a series of tones known as a tone-row. The Lyric Suite was inspired by a painful and trying incident in Berg's life – a doomed affair with a married woman. Not surprisingly, the music expresses the range of moods, from joy to passion to despair, with Romantic sensibilities still very prominent. One of Berg's strengths was that he never permitted any compositional technique or method to completely steer him. He used them, or elements of them, to help him express what he had to say.

Anton Webern followed Schoenberg into atonality more deeply than Berg did. Unlike them, Webern was very well-trained, earning a Ph.D. in Music from the University of Vienna in 1906 on the music of the Renaissance. Webern developed Schoenberg's principles by applying the serial method of composition to almost all aspects of his music – from the pitches, to their durations, tone colour, rhythms, and dynamics. He had a meticulous musical mind and laboured over his works, leaving a total output of only three hours of music.

Both Berg and Webern died of unusual causes. In the fall of 1935, Berg was stung on the lower back by an insect. An abscess developed, it was lanced, but the infection spread, eventually turning into blood poisoning. Despite operations and blood transfusions, Berg died on Christmas Eve, 1935.

Webern survived the Second World War, although his music was banned by the Nazis as degenerate. Shortly after the war ended, he visited his daughter and son-in-law. After dinner, he stepped outside on the porch for a cigarette and was shot by an occupying American soldier.

As their name suggests, the Alban Berg Quartet is no stranger to music by Schoenberg, Berg, and Webern. This is extremely difficult music to bring across and can often sound like dry, intellectual compositional exercises in the hands of inexperienced groups. But these performances clearly show the link to the nineteenth-century musical traditions, providing excitement, expression, and warmth.

■

ALBAN BERG AND ANTON WEBERN: *Music for String Quartet*
The Alban Berg Quartet
Teldec 3984-21967-2

SERGEI PROKOFIEV (1891–1953):
Romeo and Juliet (Excerpts)

Along with many other Russians, Sergei Prokofiev left his homeland after the 1917 Russian Revolution and settled abroad. Many were never to return, but Prokofiev did go back in the 1930s. His reasons have never been completely clear, but a great deal was going on that must have influenced his decision. There was a burgeoning film industry in the USSR at the time that craved musical scores. Prokofiev's sojourn in the West had not been as beneficial to his career as he had hoped. Like other Russians, including Dmitri Shostakovich (who never left), there was a feeling that for the Soviet system to really have a chance to work, there had to be a serious attempt by its citizens. But maybe more than anything else, Prokofiev was homesick. He told a friend, "The air of foreign lands does not inspire me, because I am Russian. And there is nothing more harmful to a man than to live in exile. I must hear Russian speech and talk with the people dear to me. This will give me what I lack here, for their songs are my songs. Yes, my friend, I'm going home!"

One of the first works Prokofiev composed after returning to the USSR was the ballet *Romeo and Juliet*. The project had been initiated by the Kirov Theatre in Leningrad, but for some reason, they backed out early on. Prokofiev then signed a contract with the Bolshoi Theatre in Moscow, and he wrote much of the ballet in the summer of 1935. When the Bolshoi heard the music, they declared it "undanceable" and reneged on the deal. By this time, Prokofiev was most likely having second thoughts about his decision to return to the USSR, but he did pull together some of the numbers into two concert suites, and they were successfully per-formed and received. The premiere of the ballet didn't even take place in the Soviet Union, but in the provincial Czech town of Brno in 1938, without Prokofiev's involvement. It was eventually staged in Leningrad by the Kirov early in 1940. At the cast party after the Soviet premiere, the ballerina who had danced the part of Juliet paraphrased the concluding lines of the Shakespeare play and offered the toast, "Never was a greater tale of woe, than Prokofiev's music for Romeo." Today, *Romeo and Juliet* is regarded as one of Prokofiev's finest works, and one of the jewels of the entire ballet repertoire. With it and the later *Cinderella*, both full-length ballets, Prokofiev proved that he was the Russian ballet heir to Tchaikovsky.

This 1986 recording was one of the first by the Finnish con-ductor Esa-Pekka Salonen, who was still in his twenties at the time. It made the music world take notice of this new conductor. With sumptuous and clean playing from the Berlin Philharmonic, Salonen nicely balances the tender romance of the two title char-acters with the violence between their families. The excerpts chosen follow the storyline, and the budget price only makes this recording all the more attractive.

■ ——————————————————————————

SERGEI PROKOFIEV: *Romeo and Juliet (Excerpts)*
Berlin Philharmonic Orchestra/Esa-Pekka Salonen
Sony Classical   SBK 89740

SERGEI PROKOFIEV (1891–1953):
Piano Sonata No. 7

As a student at the St. Petersburg Conservatory, Prokofiev had been a promising pianist. Promising, but also difficult and unruly. Prokofiev was something of an *enfant terrible* as a young man, a label that he enjoyed and even cultivated. He hated authority, his compositions raised the eyebrows of his teachers, he constantly questioned them about why things were done the way they were, and he poked fun at the music of past masters. After his first year at the Conservatory, his piano teacher noted, "Has assimilated little of my method. Is very talented but rather crude."

All the same, Prokofiev developed into a brilliant pianist, and the early part of his career was carved as a performer of his own piano music and he premiered his first six piano sonatas. But by the time of the Second World War and the Sonata No. 7, composing had become more important to him than performing. His pianistic skills diminished, and he left the premieres of his piano works to others.

The three piano sonatas, Nos. 6, 7, and 8 by Prokofiev, carry the collective nickname "The War Sonatas." They were all composed in the Soviet Union in the early 1940s, and express the feelings and hopes of the Soviet people during the war. The Piano Sonata No. 7 was premiered in Moscow in 1943 by pianist Sviatoslav Richter and was one of the musical highlights in the USSR during the war. The event had been discussed and anticipated for months, and most of the Moscow musical community were in attendance, including Prokofiev himself and the great Soviet violinist David Oistrakh. After Richter played the Sonata

No. 7, the hall erupted in applause. Richter was brought back again and again for curtain calls, and Prokofiev himself was called to the stage to share in the ovation. Then, after most of the audience had left, a few musicians pleaded with Richter to repeat the sonata, so that they could listen to it again, more carefully now, soaking up its powerful message and energy.

The Sonata No. 7 is a dark, ominous work, even desolate at times. The third and final movement is a real showstopper – a driving toccata with jazz influences that has sometimes been described as satanic.

Maurizio Pollini brings all the desolation and frustration of wartime to bear in his 1971 recording. Many pianists concentrate on the percussive, angular style of Prokofiev's piano music, but Pollini balances it with the less obvious lyrical side, which lies just under the surface. His phenomenal technique, stunning as it is, is always used as the servant of the music, and not for mere bravura. This recording – one of Pollini's finest – shows one of the twentieth century's greatest pianists in peak form. It is nothing short of exhilarating.

■ _____

SERGEI PROKOFIEV: *Piano Sonata No. 7*
Maurizio Pollini
DGG The Originals   447 4312

CARL ORFF (1895-1982):
Carmina Burana

The influence of Carl Orff today comes more from his role as an educator than as a composer. He worked as an opera coach and conductor in various German cities in the early part of his career, and composed music in a post-Romantic style, influenced by Richard Strauss, Arnold Schoenberg, and Impressionism. But around 1920, through collaborations with dancers, Orff became interested in the Dalcroze method of music education, or eurhythmics, which holds that music and our perception of music stem from the physical realization of its creation. By 1925, Orff and a colleague had established a music school that was based on the concept of teaching music to children in tandem with physical movement, using the basic rhythm patterns of speech as the building blocks. Eventually Orff published his *Schulwerk*, which stressed these links between music, speech, and movement. This pedagogical approach is still used around the world today.

About the same time as he founded the school, Orff took a job as conductor of the Munich Bach Society and became interested in older choral music by the likes of Monteverdi and J.S. Bach. His love and interest led him to make performing editions of this music. Then in 1935, Orff's interests were united when he was introduced to a collection of thirteenth-century poems and texts from a monastery at Beuron, near Munich. Published in the nineteenth century under the title *Carmina Burana*, or literally, "Songs of Beuron," it is a rich collection of medieval secular poetry, with insights into the feelings and aspirations of the people of the day. Orff was immediately taken by its raw, earthy qualities and vivid imagery. He set about two dozen of the texts to music. The result, one of the more popular twentieth-century works for chorus and orchestra, is the scenic cantata called *Carmina Burana*.

Orff grouped the poems into three categories: "Spring," "In the Tavern," and "The Court of Love," with the theme of Fate running throughout. The songs cover a broad range of topics and emotions – from the warmth of the spring sun to rousing drinking songs and to the many sides of love, from both female and male perspectives. Orff's aim was to strip away the over-sophistication of music to reveal its basic, primordial elements. There's an emphasis on rhythm, simple repetitive melodies, basic harmonies, and simple forms with little counterpoint. *Carmina Burana* is neither lofty nor intellectual. Its appeal has always been its directness, making it one of the most human of all works.

Eugen Jochum's recording of *Carmina Burana* from 1967 is one of the most-often recommended. Jochum was able to catch the balance between the biting sarcasm of some of the texts and the tender lyricism of others. Tenor Gerhard Stolze is wonderful in the "Ballad of the Roasted Swan," where he sings of his previous life while turning over a fire on a spit. Soprano Gundula Janowitz brings dignity and innocence to her role, while baritone Dietrich Fischer-Dieskau combines the refined approach of a great lieder singer with the gruffness and bitterness needed in the tavern songs.

■
_____

CARL ORFF: *Carmina Burana*
Gundula Janowitz, Dietrich Fischer-Dieskau, Gerhard Stolze,
    Chorus & Orchestra of the Deutsche Oper, Berlin/Eugen Jochum
DGG The Originals   447 437-2

GEORGE GERSHWIN (1898–1937):
Rhapsody in Blue

With the development of jazz in the early twentieth century, the United States could boast of a unique brand of indigenous music. Early jazz was largely an African-American form of music, but then, in the early 1920s, a movement arose to popularize jazz, making it more acceptable to white audiences, spearheaded by the classically trained bandleader Paul Whiteman. In 1924, Whiteman organized a concert at New York's Aeolian Hall called, "An Experiment in Modern Music." At the time, George Gershwin was a very successful composer of Broadway musicals, still in his twenties. Whiteman asked Gershwin to compose a concerto for piano and jazz orchestra for the concert. At first, Gershwin wrestled with the idea, but quickly saw the opportunities. He wrote, "There had been so much chatter about the limitations of jazz that I resolved to kill the misconception with one blow. The rhapsody began as a purpose, not a plan."

The piece could've easily become a dry, academic exercise in "jazzifying" classical music, or "classicalizing" jazz, with dressed-up rhythms and pseudo-improvisatory sections. But in the hands of George Gershwin, it became a masterpiece – a symbol of the entire Jazz Age, the Roaring Twenties, and the emergence of the United States onto the international scene.

Gershwin intended to title the work "American Rhapsody." It was his brother Ira, the lyricist, who came up with the more catchy *Rhapsody in Blue*. Consisting of one long movement divided into three distinct sections of fast-slow-fast (like a classical piano concerto), *Rhapsody in Blue* is a brilliant hybrid of jazz-influenced show tunes within the style of a virtuoso piano concerto by Liszt, Tchaikovsky, or Rachmaninoff. Gershwin completed the work as a two-piano version in about three weeks. It was the Paul Whiteman Band's arranger, Ferde Grofe, who orchestrated it so vividly. Gershwin himself played the solo piano part at the premiere, which at the time, had not yet been written out. The work opens with a low trill, followed by a rising, articulated run for the clarinet. At the early rehearsals, weary after hours of practising, the clarinet player improvised this opening segment, and played a glissando instead, or a smooth ascending slide. Gershwin apparently loved the effect, and the opening has been performed in this style ever since.

When Leonard Bernstein recorded *Rhapsody in Blue* with the New York Philharmonic in 1959, it was only a couple of years after the success of his hit Broadway show, *West Side Story*. Like Gershwin earlier, Bernstein had been able to synthesize the myriad of American musical styles into his own. On this recording, as piano soloist and conductor, he has a wonderful flair, flexibility, and spontaneity. It's unpredictable and aggressive, but with a warm sentiment in the slow section. *Rhapsody in Blue* was a symbol of the emergence of the United States between the wars – confident, brash, and racy – and few have captured it better than Leonard Bernstein.

■

GEORGE GERSHWIN: *Rhapsody in Blue*
Leonard Bernstein, Columbia Symphony Orchestra
Sony Classical   SMK 63086

AARON COPLAND (1900–1990): *Appalachian Spring*

To many music lovers, the composer Aaron Copland almost defines American classical music. He started his career as a composer by studying with the famous musical pedagogue Nadia Boulanger in Paris and, not surprisingly, his music at the time was strongly influenced by the avant-garde of European music. It was edgy, with clean lines and textures, something like the neoclassical works of Igor Stravinsky. But in the 1930s, back home in the U.S., Copland changed course. He believed, as he said later, that, "a new public for music had grown up around radio and the phonograph. It made no sense to ignore them. I felt it was worth the effort to say what I had to say in the simplest possible terms."

Copland's music became less complex and more accessible. He incorporated the melodies and rhythms of American folk music, jazz, and popular music into his own. It was a music that sounded fresh and contemporary, and yet at the same time, familiar and comfortable.

After the success of the two "western" ballets, *Billy the Kid* and *Rodeo*, Copland was commissioned by dancer Martha Graham in 1943 to write a third ballet. American patriotism and optimism surrounding the Second World War were running high, and the ballet would tell the story of a bride and groom setting up their new farmhouse in the hills of Pennsylvania in the early nineteenth century. By the end, the new couple is seen strong and sturdy, as they face their future together. It was a story of hope and promise, confidence and faith, and it holds many of the feelings and aspirations – both personal and as a nation – of the American people during the war. By using American folk music idioms and styles, Copland created a work that sounded distinctly "American." He even used "The Gift to Be Simple," a tune of the nineteenth-century American religious sect known as the Shakers as the basis of a series of variations in the ballet. For the premiere at the Library of Congress in Washington, D.C., in 1944, Copland was limited by space and had to score *Appalachian Spring* for just thirteen players. It forced him to concentrate on varieties of textures and tone colours, and the interplay between lines of music, which only enhanced the vitality of the ballet. A year after the premiere, Copland created a suite of the music for full orchestra, which still maintains the clarity of texture. It's this orchestral suite that is usually heard today.

No one could hold a candle to Leonard Bernstein in the realm of American orchestral music during his tenure at the helm of the New York Philharmonic Orchestra in the 1950s and '60s. A composer himself, Bernstein seemed to know instinctively how American music should go. It was lively, brash, and assertive at times, and yet tender and lyrical at others. And, as well as the knowledge of how it should go, there was Bernstein's deep love for the music and the topic. Aaron Copland conducted and recorded *Appalachian Spring* himself, but even he was not able to capture the emotions and impressions that Leonard Bernstein brought to this great score.

■————————————————————————————————————

 AARON COPLAND: *Appalachian Spring*
New York Philharmonic Orchestra/Leonard Bernstein
Sony Classical   SMK 63082

DMITRI SHOSTAKOVICH (1906–1975): *Symphonies No. 5 and No. 9*

The music of Soviet composer Dmitri Shostakovich has become very controversial in recent years. Shostakovich lived his entire life under the Soviet regime, and his story is a grim but fascinating study into the struggles an artist must endure under totalitarian rule. As a prominent Soviet composer during the Stalin era, Shostakovich had a roller-coaster ride. One year, he would be awarded top Soviet honours as a model composer glorifying the state and representing the aspirations of the proletariat. The next, his music would be lambasted as chaos. The whim of Stalin's cultural policy would have changed, Shostakovich would be publicly disgraced and forced to apologize. Shortly after his death in 1975, many adopted the view that Shostakovich was, in reality, a lifelong dissident, who secretly encoded anti-communist messages in his music. It was believed that he had led a double life – on the surface he had toed the communist party line and did as he was told, but in reality, in the secret life of his music, his real beliefs and feelings were told. There have been several books written both presenting and challenging this idea, so a fair amount of confusion still exists today. Without a doubt, Shostakovich lived a frustrating life, but like any great composer, he caught and reflected his times and the feelings of the people around him. All we really have is his music to tell us, and, as always, it's the best representation of the message.

The Symphony No. 5 by Shostakovich was composed in the 1930s during the terrible years of the Stalin purges. Shostakovich had been at the high point of his roller-coaster life, after the success of the opera *Lady Macbeth of Mtsensk*. But Stalin and his cultural authorities denounced the opera as "muddle," Shostakovich was disgraced and forced to apologize publicly. The Symphony No. 5, he said, was composed as "a Soviet artist's response to just criticism." In it, Shostakovich traces a journey from darkness and oppression to a triumphant conclusion. Or so it seemed, anyway. Some feel that the victory is hollow and false – that Shostakovich was merely placating his bosses. Regardless of point of view, the symphony can, and does, work brilliantly as pure music.

The Symphony No. 9 was supposed to be a work of victory, composed and first performed at the end of the Second World War. But, again the message is veiled. The scaled-down performing forces and the witty nature of the work seem to lead to another victory – the kind of thing the Soviet cultural authorities would have wanted. But, as in the Symphony No. 5, the victory seems to lack sincerity and commitment.

Conductor Bernard Haitink recorded all fifteen symphonies by Shostakovich for Decca with the London Philharmonic and Concertgebouw Orchestras. The Symphonies Nos. 5 and 9, both here on one disc, are two of the cycle's highlights. Haitink distinguishes himself by ignoring the controversies and supposed hidden meanings, and presents straightforward accounts, allowing the music to stand on its own. The symphonies plumb emotional depths and rise to lofty heights, letting the listener decide the message.

■

DMITRI SHOSTAKOVICH: *Symphonies No. 5 and No. 9*
Concertgebouw Orchestra of Amsterdam, London Philharmonic
    Orchestra/Bernard Haitink
Decca Eloquence   467 478-2

DMITRI SHOSTAKOVICH (1906–1975):
String Quartets Nos. 1, 8, 9

The symphonies by Soviet composer Dmitri Shostakovich were a very public and political form of music, especially during the Stalin era, when all eyes and ears were on the composer. It is music that lays out the message and emotions his Soviet bosses wanted to hear. The chamber music by Shostakovich is much more intimate, sometimes autobiographical, expressing his personal responses to some of the events taking place in the world around him. The string quartets trace a thread through his creative life, from the beginnings of his troubles with the Stalin authorities in the 1930s, to his death in 1975. Many believe that Shostakovich's most private feelings are expressed in his fifteen string quartets. They certainly contain Shostakovich's distinct style and sound, and are among the finest chamber music pieces composed during the twentieth century.

Composed in the late 1930s, shortly after the Symphony No. 5, the String Quartet No. 1 seems relaxed and light-humoured. Shostakovich himself called it a "springtime work." But underneath the smooth surface, there's a quiet uneasiness and tension.

The Quartet No. 8 is the most popular of the fifteen. The inspiration for the Quartet comes from 1960 when Shostakovich was in Dresden working on a film score for a Soviet documentary on the Second World War. The destruction and devastation of the German city, which had been fire-bombed, reminded him of his own war years in the USSR. It made such an impression on him that he completed the String Quartet No. 8 in a mere three days. By using a musical theme in which the notes form an acronym of his surname, and quoting from some of his earlier works, Shostakovich created an autobiographical composition that is intense and anguished. Not surprisingly, it was one of the works performed at his funeral in 1975. The quartet is one of the most gripping examples of a composer's personal comment on the futility of war.

The Quartet No. 9 was composed a few years after the Eighth, although Shostakovich had worked on it for some time. He described an early version of the quartet as a children's work, based on themes from his own childhood. But depressed and lacking self-confidence at the time, it seems he burned at least one, and possibly two, early versions of the work before settling on the final score, something he hadn't done since his student days.

The musicians of the Eder Quartet bring a tight, blended sound to their complete transversal of the Shostakovich Quartets for Naxos, available on single CDs of two or three quartets each. They reach the emotional heart of this music, very aware of the circumstances behind the compositions and the personality of the composer and his intentions. The sound is bright and present, and at a budget price, this recording easily beats its competitors.

■

DMITRI SHOSTAKOVICH: *String Quartets Nos. 1, 8, 9*
Eder Quartet
Naxos 8.550973

OLIVIER MESSIAEN (1908–1992):
Turangalîla Symphony

One of the greatest composers of the twentieth century, and one of the most influential, was Olivier Messiaen. Even from his first published work in 1929, Messiaen showed he was a musician of incredible originality and innovation.

After studying at the Paris Conservatoire with such notables as composer Paul Dukas and organist Marcel Dupré, Messiaen took a prominent church organist's job in Paris and planned for a career as an organist, composer, and teacher. But his goals and ambitions were greater, and although he maintained the organist's position for decades, Messiaen branched out into various musical endeavours. The Second World War interrupted his life, but even it wasn't able to take him completely off track. Messiaen was called up, served, was captured and imprisoned as a P.O.W. While in Stalag VIIIA in Silesia, he composed the *Quartet for the End of Time*, for clarinet, violin, cello, and piano – the only available instruments in the camp. The work is a moving, gripping testament to the tragedy of war and its effects.

After the war, Messiaen settled back into life in Paris, returned to his organist's position and accepted a teaching job at the Conservatoire. He was a brilliant teacher and influenced many musicians and composers, including Pierre Boulez, Karlheinz Stockhausen, Iannis Xenakis, William Albright, and the pianist Yvonne Loriod, who became his second wife in 1962.

Messiaen was like a sponge when it came to music. He absorbed a huge array of influences, from plainchant to Debussy, Stravinsky, and Schoenberg, from traditional Asian music to bird song. He once said, "An abundance of technical means allows the heart to expand." Although he never belonged to any musical school, his devout Catholicism was always a dominant part of his life and music.

Messiaen's sincerity and the trust in him it inspired is clear in a letter for one of his commissions. In 1945, the conductor of the Boston Symphony Orchestra, Serge Koussevitzky, asked Messiaen for an orchestral work, with the following stipulations: "Write me the work you want to, in the style you want, as long as you want, with the instrumental formation you want." The *Turangalîla* Symphony was the result, a sprawling ten-movement piece for an orchestra of more than one hundred players, including a huge percussion section. The title, pronounced Too-rahn-ger-*lee*-lah, comes from Sanskrit and means the game of life and death, love, and time. At its core, the work deals with the universal concept of love and death. Messiaen himself called it a love song. Despite its length of almost an hour and a half, and a complex musical language, the *Turangalîla* Symphony has always been popular with audiences.

There's a spontaneous excitement and sense of adventure in this recording led by the Polish conductor Antoni Wit. The huge orchestra is well-balanced, bringing across Messiaen's fabulous sense of orchestral sonority and colour. The epic quality of the work as a whole – often a challenge for interpreters – holds together well, for a powerful impact. Also included on this recording is the early spiritual work for orchestra, "L'Ascension."

■ ———————————————————————————————————————

OLIVIER MESSIAEN: *Turangalîla Symphony*
Polish National Radio Symphony Orchestra/Antoni Wit
Naxos 8.554 478/9

BENJAMIN BRITTEN (1913–1976): War Requiem, Op. 66

Throughout history, artists have created works of art that have commented on the eternal topic of war. Whether describing the fears of people in wartime, triumphant victory, or warnings, and prayers for peace, composers have commented on and criticized war for centuries. The protest song existed long before Woody Guthrie, Pete Seeger, and Bob Dylan.

The English composer Benjamin Britten was a lifelong pacifist. Growing up on the east coast of England, some of Britten's earliest memories as a boy were of the sound of German bombs exploding during the First World War. Just before the Second World War broke out, he left England for Canada and the United States. Although he remained a conscientious objector for the rest of the war, he returned to England in 1942 to help in the war effort. Britten wrestled with the concepts of morals, ethics, and conscientiousness within the expectations of society, and such works as his operas *Peter Grimes* and *Billy Budd* deal with the subject of the outcast in society. But Britten's most powerful statement is his *War Requiem*.

In 1940, German bombers destroyed the fourteenth-century Coventry Cathedral in England. A new one was built right beside the shattered remains, and Benjamin Britten was asked to compose a work for its consecration. He jumped at the chance, because he saw it as a way to denounce the futility and waste of war, while marking England's recovery from the war's destruction. By combining the text of the ancient Latin Requiem Mass for the Dead with antiwar poetry by the British poet Wilfred Owen (1893–1918),

Britten created a work for all time that condemns war while pushing for hope and reconciliation. Wilfred Owen had been a gifted poet – a decorated English army officer killed in action in the First World War at the age of twenty-five, one week before the armistice in 1918. On the title page of the *War Requiem*, Britten used the words of the poet Owen. "My subject is War, and the pity of War. The Poetry is in the pity. All a poet can do is warn." The first performance of the *War Requiem* was in May 1962 at the consecration of the new St. Michael's Cathedral in Coventry. The work was immediately successful and has rightfully become one of the great choral works of any age.

Britten organized the *War Requiem* into three planes. Out front are the tenor and baritone soloists, singing the poems of Wilfred Owen and representing an English and German soldier, respectively. One of the most gripping moments of the piece is when the English soldier meets the German he killed the day before, in the vague confines of death. The German says to him, "Whatever hope is yours, was my life also . . . I am the enemy you killed, my friend/ I knew you in this dark: for so you frowned/ Yesterday through me as you jabbed and killed/ I parried; but my hands were loath and cold/ Let us sleep now."

In the middle plane are the large choir, soprano soloist, and orchestra. They present the Latin Mass for the Dead. The third plane is in the background, or sometimes up in a choir loft. The boys' choir and organ, sounding like the far-off voices of angels, sing mostly the Latin Requiem text, and mostly when it deals with death and life-after-death. The juxtaposition of the Latin Requiem text, with the antiwar poems, within the three musical planes is nothing short of brilliant, and results in a work of incredible statement, power, and effect.

Although several good recordings of the *War Requiem* have been made, none can surpass the gripping intensity of the composer's own, recorded in 1963, within a year of the premiere. The three soloists were the three Britten intended for the work, representing three of the nations that suffered the most in the Second World War – the Russian soprano Galina Vishnevskaya, the English tenor (and Britten's partner) Peter Pears, and the German baritone Dietrich Fischer-Dieskau. Performance standard, sound quality, and impact have made this a legendary recording.

■ _____

BENJAMIN BRITTEN: *War Requiem, Op. 66*
Galina Vishnevskaya, Dietrich Fischer-Dieskau, Peter Pears,
   Melos Ensemble, London Symphony Orchestra & Chorus,
   etc./Benjamin Britten
Decca   414 383-2

LEONARD BERNSTEIN (1918–1990):
Candide Overture, West Side Story Symphonic Dances, etc.

Leonard Bernstein epitomized the American approach to classical music in the mid-twentieth century. Bright, talented, confident, brash, showy, even arrogant, Bernstein broke with time-honoured musical traditions, capturing the heartbeat of the United States. Just as Canada's Glenn Gould was, Bernstein was originally viewed by the European musical establishment as lightweight and eccentric – his music a flashy trend or fad that would soon pass. Even some American critics and music lovers thought Bernstein lacked musical substance and worth, but they were proven wrong. As Bernstein's career progressed, it became clear that here was a musician with incredible talents – as a pianist, conductor, educator, writer, and composer.

Leonard Bernstein was the first prominent American musician to be born and trained in the United States. Prior to him, U.S. orchestras tended to hire European musicians to lead them, or Americans who had been trained in Europe in the proper methods of classical music. Bernstein had been schooled at Harvard University and the Curtis Institute of Music in Philadelphia. He was a protegé of the conductors Serge Koussevitzky of the Boston Symphony Orchestra and later Dmitri Mitropoulos of the New York Philharmonic. He got his big break in 1943, when he filled in at short notice for an ailing Bruno Walter, in a New York Philharmonic concert. The next day, the word of Bernstein's conducting debut was front-page news. The *New York Times* called it "a good American success story." Here was an American musician in his mid-twenties, who had conquered the seemingly cold and impenetrable European world of classical music. Even more important maybe, was that Bernstein seemed quintessentially American – a jazz-playing, apple-pie-eating, boy-next-door type done good. Bernstein's star continued to rise. In 1957, *West Side Story*, his most popular work opened on Broadway, and a year later, he was appointed to the helm of the New York Philharmonic Orchestra. Some loved him, some hated him, but like him or not, he couldn't be ignored. By the 1960s, he had become the most prominent and powerful musical figure in the country and one of the world's most famous conductors. His popularity was so great that when President John F. Kennedy met Bernstein, he told him, "You're the only man I know I would never run against."

Bernstein's great gift was his ability to absorb and assimilate the myriad of musical influences that were prevalent in contemporary American culture. They included classical music, jazz, Broadway, rock-and-roll, and earlier American music by the likes of George Gershwin and Aaron Copland. But his most popular music, like *West Side Story*, led many people to view him primarily as a composer of lighter music, and throughout his life Bernstein struggled with the stigma. He wanted so much to be recognized as a great, "serious" musician, and it's only since his death in 1990, and the huge swell of reissues of his recordings, that he has come to be properly recognized and valued internationally.

In American music, and especially his own, Bernstein had few competitors. And although he re-recorded much of his music later in his career, it's his early recordings from the 1950s and '60s that are the finest. At the time, *West Side Story* and *Candide*, a comic operetta, were viewed as groundbreaking. Bernstein's dash and flair, as well as the crisp rhythms and tight ensemble of his New York Philharmonic combined to make ageless recordings that may never be bettered.

■ ───────────────────────────────────────

LEONARD BERNSTEIN: *Candide Overture, West Side Story
   Symphonic Dances, etc.*
New York Philharmonic Orchestra/Leonard Bernstein
Sony Classical   SMK 63085

ARVO PÄRT (b. 1935):
Fratres

One of the most popular living composers is the Estonian Arvo Pärt. Born in 1935, he graduated from the Tallinn Conservatory in 1963, while working as a recording engineer in the music department at Estonian Radio. Pärt's early works show the influence of Russian and Soviet music by Sergei Prokofiev and Dmitri Shostakovich, but by 1960 he had adopted the serial techniques developed by Arnold Schoenberg. Losing interest quickly, he then tried his hand at collage techniques, quoting from existing music by J.S. Bach and others. This, too, didn't hold his attention for long, and he entered into one of several periods of study and contemplation. Pärt immersed himself in music by the medieval and Renaissance masters like Machaut, Ockeghem, Obrecht, and Josquin, as well as music of the Orthodox Church. By the mid-1970s, he was composing again, but in a new style with a mystical, spiritual feel inspired by plainchant and Renaissance polyphony. Pärt called it "tintinnabulation," after the Latin for little bells, saying, "I have discovered that it is enough when a single note is beautifully played. This one note, or a silent beat, or a moment of silence, comforts me. I work with very few elements – with one voice, with two voices. I build with the most primitive materials – with the triad, with one specific tonality. The three notes of a triad are like bells. And that is why I call it tintinnabulation."

The premise behind Pärt's technique is the treatment of two parts as one. One part moves stepwise to and from a central point, while the other sounds the notes of the triad. The result is music that moves very slowly, repeating and unfolding as time goes on, with an almost hypnotic effect. *Fratres*, or "Brothers" is one such work, composed in 1977 and subsequently adapted for any number of solo and ensemble combinations of winds, strings, and percussion. In it, a stark, chorale-like tune is heard over a continuous drone, like that of a bagpipe. Simple percussion adds punctuation. As *Fratres* progresses, the tune is repeated, each time lower in pitch, until a rich sonority is achieved. The piece works toward a musical climax, backs away from it, then returns as it began. *Fratres* has caught the imagination of many who search for spirituality and meaning in today's hectic world. It's a work that soothes and calms in a regulatory, structured way, not unlike the church music of the great Renaissance masters – creating an oasis of calm, in which many find stimulation and refreshment. The six different versions of *Fratres* featured on the recommended recording help to prove that strong material can be reworked, over and over again, successfully, just with the simple variation of colours and textures.

This Telarc recording with I Fiamminghi, The Orchestra of Flanders, combines excellent playing with the proper atmosphere and mood. The music of Pärt can easily disintegrate into merely endless repetitions, if concentration lags. I Fiamminghi does not allow that to happen, and the rich but clear recorded sound only adds to the music's soothing and sensual beauty.

■ ───

ARVO PÄRT: *Fratres*
I Fiamminghi
Telarc CD-80387

INDEX